PATRICK LEDWELL

The Acorn Press
Charlottetown
2016

ACORNPRESS

P.O. Box 22024
Charlottetown, Prince Edward Island
C1A 9J2
acornpresscanada.com

Printed and Bound in Canada

Edited by David Malahoff

Copy edit by Jane Ledwell

Digital composite graphics designed and created by Patrick Ledwell

Cover illustration by Jeff Alward

Design and layout by Matt Reid

Library and Archives Canada Cataloguing in Publication

Ledwell, Patrick, 1973-, author
 An islander strikes back / Patrick Ledwell.

Issued in print and electronic formats.
ISBN 978-1-927502-25-9 (pbk.).--ISBN 978-1-927502-26-6 (ebook)

 1. Ledwell, Patrick, 1973-. 2. Prince Edward Island--Humor.
3. Canadian wit and humor (English)--Prince Edward Island.
I. Title.

PS8623.E4324I75 2014   C818'.602   C2014-903536-5
                                               C2014-903537-3

   Canada Council for the Arts   Conseil des Arts du Canada

Funded by the Government of Canada

We acknowledge the [financial] support of the Government of Canada, the Canada Council for the Arts and the Province of Prince Edward Island.

To my wife Tara and my son Nate.

You're my forever family.

Introduction

I think we're drawn to stories where people are hanging on.

Starting from the early eighties, the *Star Wars* trilogy took up ninety-eight per cent of my developing brain. And *The Empire Strikes Back* was my favourite, although it's the middle one, full of disappointments.

Starting out, the scrappy band of rebels barely survive on a hostile ice planet. Han Solo gets betrayed and frozen alive in a block of carbonite. Luke Skywalker returns too quickly from swampland training to face Darth Vader, who turns out to be his father. And then Vader cuts Luke's hand off. Thanks a ton, Dad.

Pretty dark matter for an eight-year-old.

But the movie hit me where I lived, on Prince Edward Island at that time. The hostile ice planet was a special gift to the imagination. There was a series of bad winters, and I spent most of them encased in a snow cave, pretending I was surviving storms in the carved out belly of my slain drift-striding creature.

So when I started putting together pieces for this second collection, the "strikes back" tag suggested itself, and that's no surprise.

The Empire Strikes Back is a ridiculous space Western, I know. But it does have some themes that resonate past its industrial light and magic. Survival against the elements. Trying to get back home. The mystery of fatherhood.

And these questions were the big ones for me when I was trying to put this book together. In a whirlwind couple of weeks, in fall 2012, our son Nathaniel was born and we moved back to my family homestead in rural PEI. The first pieces in the book date from that same time.

A couple of the winters since have been some of the fiercest on record. They've sometimes left us wondering why we set up base on this ice island. Nothing like getting pushed back to help you find your ground.

I've written most of these pieces in the dark, either early mornings or late nights. Comedy's been a belly that I can crawl into, to recharge and face whatever other winds are howling. The pieces are not serious. They're the opposite. There are ridiculous pictures of shopping bags and gympants, and bundles of real newspaper clippings. There are debates where I was assigned a ridiculous position in advance. If I can keep you distracted and happy for three pages, mission accomplished.

That said, I hope the last few intense, special years made it in here, somehow.

Patrick
January, 2016

PEI PROS AND CONS

PEI Pros and Cons

Living on an Island is different.

The borders are no floating negotiations between neighbours. They're as real as walking off a cliff.

You're either on the Island or off it. That much is clear. But the reasons to stay or go are anything but well defined.

I have an internal battle between the things that keep me rooted and the things that make me think I should uproot, for good.

Every couple of months, I decide it's time to get perspective, using a small exercise of mine. I take a pen, usually from a local hotel. I divide a piece of paper down the middle and write down PEI pros on one side and PEI cons on the other.

PEI Pros

You don't have to lock your doors.

A husband on a ride-on for two full days has saved many marriages.

If you want affordable oceanfront, just buy a cottage across the road in a field, and wait.

Islanders have a relaxed attitude toward fashion.

PEI Cons

Have a look in our house. What's worth stealing?

Gigantic lawns that take the whole weekend to cut.

The Island is eroding at a rate of a metre per year.

When you wear your pyjama pants to the Superstore, pull them the hell up, at least.

PEI Pros

Staff at the pharmacy call you "dear" and know what you're picking up.

We volunteer time and time again.

Our accent adds resonance to our speech.

PEI Cons

People behind you in line at the pharmacy call you "dear" and read your prescription off the bag.

We wear the volunteer jackets, time and time again, for more than two decades after the event. Hello there, 1991 Canada Games.

Our accent adds consonants to words where they don't belong. "This is my cousint. In hockey, he plays goaldie. Leave your kitbag in the garajsh, until you get it warshed."

Are we still calling this English?

I should go. The pro I hired to install our oil tank I'm starting to think may be a con. I knew his sister back in junior high.

Road Signs of the Island

Island friends, summer eventually pushes through the pavement. Time to have that Impala inspected and get out on the highways and byways of Prince Edward Island. Does "byway" mean a divided highway? If so, on the Island, you'll need to settle for just highways.

Only in urbane places like Moncton do roads go both ways. Islanders drive all together just fine, like long-married people who know each other's moves. A couple tentative turn-ons, and after that stay over on your own side, old coot.

However, during the summer, it's important to remember that visitors motor to the Island from all over North America and attempt to drive among us. Not all of these people grew up alongside you and your patterns. They don't know you always play cards with Wayne on Wednesday, and so turn abruptly 'round about his place. You should follow some rules and deploy your turn signal, during these unique summer times.

Let's reconnoitre ourselves with a few conventional signs of the road.

That other half of the road voted differently

What does this sign mean? Clear enough. When you see this sign, get prepared for an unceremonious farewell to pavement. The drop-off will coincide with the mailbox where the local voting pattern shifted. You'd think communities would catch on, vote strategically as a block, and get the road paved smooth to the end.

People Supported by Shovel

Contrary to popular fears, this sign does not announce a noisy round of construction. Look closely. No human can lift a shovel leaning at that impossible forty-five degree angle out from that part of the midsection. The shovel is there for support. These zones are designed to slow traffic to prevent gravel noise from disturbing the sleep of anyone in adjacent areas.

Speaking of standing by the road, you should watch out for these signs because PEI is very pedestrian. And not always on purpose. Once when my car was in the shop for the morning, three separate people asked me, "Saw you walking. Everything going okay?"

At any rate, pedestrians don't deserve any bruises, other than to their pride. Drivers, the white lines on the road are not there so you can line pedestrians up better in your sights. Slow down. The signs recommend "Reduce Speed," rather than full stop. Use enough speed to get up in a pedestrian's grill about who owns the road. But not so much speed that you have insurance adjusters picking pedestrian out of your car's actual grill.

Await more instructions from On-Car Guidance System

Islanders are good at exercising judgment, if not other forms of exercising. When it comes to stop signs, they're an option to be taken strongly into consideration. Mainly by people who do not know the lay of the land as well as ourselves.

Many of us Islanders have lived our lives within a kilometre of a particular stop sign, like faithful dogs pegged to a stake. The most we'll agree to do is crane our necks out, to get a better whiff of what's ahead on the trail.

Besides, long-married people on PEI have an on-car system for telling them what to do that's more reliable than signs. It's your partner, sitting passenger-side, providing a non-stop, in-ear commentary of everything you just did wrong. "Didn't you see the stop sign back there? As I live and breathe, if they put your brain in a bird, it would fly backwards."

Wife no help as man misses stop sign

The man in question said that his wife is very observe he didn't believe he had vant when she's in the car gone through a stop sign with him and if he makes a because his wife did not yell mistake she will tell him so. at him.

"She didn't yell at me," he

He told Chief Provincial said.
Court Judge ▓▓▓ ▓▓▓▓▓

The safety measure of the on-car spouse is so failsafe, it's used as a defense in Island courts. This real newspaper headline is plucked straight from our halls of justice. "I ask the court," cross-examines this actual defendant, "How could the stop sign exist, when my wife in the car did not tear a strip off me for missing it?"

All in all, road signs are good fence posts, reminding Islanders that we can't always just drive how we feel.

So until next time, leave your left-turn signal on for most of the day, and stay open for possibilities.

The Debate: Is the West Coast Canada's Best Coast?

My answer: Frig off.

West Coasters are like Birkenstock sandals. They're open-toed and open-souled, and they pick up a little bit of whatever they walk through. They bring a funky smell into the room. Fair enough. East Coasters are like rubber boots. Unchanging, unfashionable, and not prepared to absorb much of anything. But you can count on us when the rains come.

Some are impressed by the Pacific salmon, which returns to the same spot every year to spawn. That pales next to the courage of the Atlantic salmon. It swims all the way up the Athabasca River to Fort McMurray, works all winter, and ships cheques back home to keep the spawn in minivans and minor hockey. That's true courage.

The West Coast has the potlatch, where one family, clan, or village overwhelms the neighbours with gifts. On the East Coast, we have the potluck. That's where you shred two bucks' worth of carrots into some green Jell-o, and then go eat the more expensive things your neighbours have brought.

We're simpler people, with simple and direct tastes.

I worked as a barista in a Halifax café that sold these pretentious, rock-hard Italian cookies called biscotti. A Cape Bretoner came back to return his. I said "It's called a biscotti, and you dunk it in your coffee." He replied, "It's a goddam stale cookie. And you can stick it up your arse."

Sure, the East Coast seems behind the times. Out here, food still becomes fusion cuisine just by adding nacho cheese.

But the East Coast is a gentler place – where a needle exchange can still occasionally be a place to trade crochet supplies.

You need to live here to understand the beauty of an East Coast spring. We have fifty shades of grey, and I don't mean that filthy metrosexual novel popular in Vancouver.

If *Fifty Shades of Grey* were written on the East Coast, the line "Anna, fix me straps and snap off me rubbers" would not even be filthy at all. Because the characters would be talking about a pair of hip-waders and how best to remove them.

Yes, Vancouver can be a beautiful setting for films, if they're about mould and light-deprivation.

But write me out of that script. I was East Coast born, I'm East Coast bred, and in a couple decades, I'll be East Coast dead. Likely of causes related to living on the East Coast.

So help me, squid-jiggin' God.

GOOD
FENCES

Waste Watch Sorting Guide

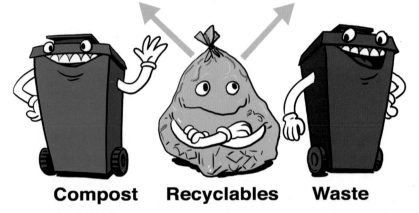

Waste Watch : #1 or #2?

Compost   **Recyclables**   **Waste**

"What day is it today?"

It's a question that echoes across Island yards, early on spring mornings. The question is not about days of the week, but whether it's a green-cart day or a black-cart day. "Green?" "Black?" Or whatever colour this coffin-sized Tupperware is supposed to be, that I'm hauling over snowbanks in the half-light.

Usually, I just look up and down the road to see what cart my neighbours have already hauled out.

Fact: There is one senior who is keeping track of what cart day it is, for the entire Island. Georgina Carruthers of Marshfield. She has the actual print calendar taped to her cupboard and puts the right cart out the night before. If she ever loses track, the entire system will tip like dominoes in the wrong direction, heaven help us all.

Our modern Waste Watch system has changed the simple act of throwing something out into a garbage game show. I see people caught in separation anxiety above the multiple bins. The contestant has a drinking box or plastic picnic fork suspended in mid-air, face contorted, unable to decide whether he needs to #1 or #2. Many tourists just put all their waste in their car trunk and drive to New Brunswick to throw the whole load out.

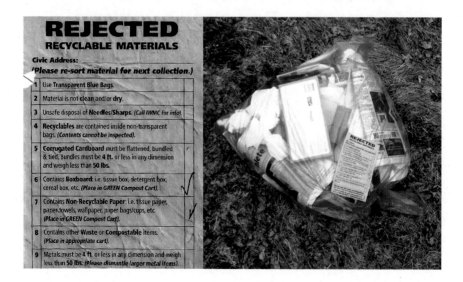

Like many Islanders, I've experienced the sting of having my blue bags rejected at roadside pickup, for improper sorting of a toilet paper roll. It's hard to express the shame of having my bags tagged and left there with a bright report card for all the neighbours to see. Failing at garbage was not a red-letter day for my self-esteem.

I've been learning Waste Watch in this trial-by-fire method for the last twenty years. To save you being similarly tagged, let's share smart strategies for sorting.

Let's begin with a basic item – our Island newspaper. After reading all three pages, the paper should be placed in blue bag #1, for paper. Unless the newspaper's been rain-soaked in the kitty litter mail bucket that you've been using since the snowplow knocked the box off. Once wet, newspaper goes in the green compost bin. Moisture releases the fertilizer woven into the fibre of Island news, and the damp paper becomes great for the potatoes.

You're ready to advance to the next level – a can of beans. There's also some concealed bacon fat in the can, because you can't go whipping hot fat directly into the green cart. Let's scrape that fat out with a corrugated beer-box flap, bundle and tie with some twine, and leave out separately by the road.

Waste Watch : Can Handling

Compost

Bag #2

The bean can is ready to begin its journey toward blue bag #2, for metal and plastic.

Before putting the empty bean can into blue bag #2, it's important to wash it very thoroughly. The industrial machine that flattens and melts metal cans cannot handle any bean residue. A single baked bean can break the molten-hot can smelter. This is a well-known fact. As you wash the can, the gluey label becomes wet, so you know what to do. Peel it off and put it in compost, because it has become great for the potatoes.

Continue washing the inside of the can, and give your hand a good, solid cut with the pizza-cutter sharpness of the hanging lid. This is pretty much unavoidable. You'll notice the dishwater changing colour.

Waste Watch : Band-Aid Solution

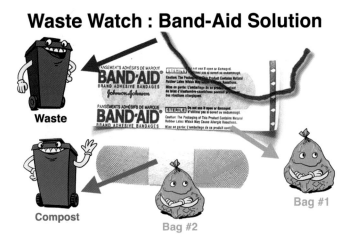

Run around frantically looking for a Band-Aid in the kitchen drawers, holding your bleeding hand in a dishtowel. Once you find and open the Band-Aid with your good hand, the wrapper of the Band-Aid is paper, so sort that into blue bag #1. The little red string that helps you split open the Band-Aid wrapper is full of red dye, which is not great for the potatoes. Pop outside and put the red string separately in the black cart, for waste.

Once your bleeding is staunched, place the clean bean can in blue bag #2.

In two weeks, when your hand is fully healed, carefully remove and separate the Band-Aid. Place the plastic Band-Aid backing in blue bag #2. Separate the cotton swab and sort that into compost.

Because your blood and tears are good for preserving the Island soil, don't you know. That is the entire concept behind Waste Watch. You've won.

The Debate: Should We Make More of an Effort to Get to Know our Neighbours?

My answer: No, get off my porch.

Take a largish raccoon. Pull him upright and shave him. Give him a bungalow and a Hyundai. And, ta-dah, you have your average Canadian neighbour. Want to get to know him better?

Yes, of course, he goes through your garbage. It's what he was born to do. And if you feed him even once, he's going to be on your damn deck every Saturday night for all of time. Even a raccoon has a better instinct to wash his hands, once in a while, while digging into nacho dip.

I come from Prince Edward Island. PEI stands for "Privacy Ends Immediately."

On the Island, privacy is threatened by social not-working. That's where your neighbours do not work regularly and devote their free time to peering through the curtains at your house.

Does this Neighbourhood Watch provide anyone with a sense of security? No. Neighbours will watch as hooded figures yank a flat screen out of your house and wonder, "When did they get one bigger than ours? I didn't see that box when I was going through their garbage."

In case you think I'm just a hayseed, I did live in Atlanta for three years. It's like Toronto, with no public transit, unconcealed racism, and open-carry weapons. That goes about as well as it sounds, neighbour-wise.

I did admire how the U.S. invested billions to determine what you *actually* need to know about your neighbours. When talking to neighbours, I say keep your conversation to the same questions a Canadian gets asked by U.S. airport security. "Are you running a drug operation?" "Do you have a concerning stockpile of firecrackers, unregistered alcohol, or off-label fruit?"

No?

"Okay, take off your shoes and come in for a tiny while. Tell me precisely when you are planning to leave."

All civilization exists pretty much to keep neighbours out of your business. You know who agrees with me? A little book called the Bible. Perhaps you've heard tell of it.

The Ten Commandments are the first restrictive covenants about how to behave in a suburban development without constantly wanting to harm your neighbours.

"Thou shalt not covet thy neighbour's goods." So when thou borrowedest my hedge trimmer last October, thou shouldst have returned it unto me, a year later.

"Thou shalt not covet thy neighbour's wife." So when I sayest, "Drop in some time," thou shalt not show up Saturday on the deck, without your wife and kids, wearing only those seventies tennis shorts. Get thee home and use my hedge trimmer to shave some shrubbery back from that banana-hammock.

I say good fences make good neighbours. And if you can afford it, buy electric.

If PEI Ruled the World:
The Google

If PEI ruled the world, Google would be renamed "The Google," because that's what we call it on the Island. And that name would refer not only to the search engine, but to all of the Internet.

Walk into an average bed-and-breakfast on PEI and ask, "Do you have wi-fi?" You will immediately receive a blank lack of recognition from the desk clerk's face. No signal whatsoever.

Instead, you should wiggle your fingers in front of the clerk and say, "Do you have The Google?" The front desk will point you to the outlet where you can jack into a fresh, flowing supply of The Google. We have a boatload.

If PEI ruled the world, our search results on The Google would be far more helpful and reliable.

As it stands now, if I go to your garden-variety Google and type in "pei," my search goes off the rails from the start. The search box tries to guess what I'm after before I have a chance to finish. I just typed a "p." Calm your nerves, The Google. You don't know if I mean "pizza" or "Pandora's box" or "pirate pants." It's too soon to tell.

It gets worse from there.

The current Google suggests all kinds of different possible pei's that distract searchers from our actual important one. Things like "percutaneous ethanol injection." I tried that once at a high school field party, and it was probably the worst time ever. Things like "preparedness exercise issue." That is not an issue on the Island, because we often wear stretchy pants. We are very prepared to potentially exercise, should a spontaneous game of dodge ball break out at the grocery store.

Person from PEI

Shar PEI puppy

Our province's biggest search overlap problem is with Shar-Pei puppies.

Say you're a possible visitor searching how to visit PEI, and instead Google trots these puppy pictures across your trail. So desperate lovable, you completely forget wanting to visit our gentle little sandbar. You're lost in the endless folds of cuteness. You wind up looking at pictures of puppies for six hours at work, get fired from your job, and then don't have the budget to travel.

If PEI ruled the world, we could create The Google that didn't mix up our province with wrinkly canines.

People from PEI have nothing in common with Shar-Pei puppies. Shar-Pei puppies are chunky and wrinkly. Once you pet one, you want to bring one home forever. People from PEI are more independent than that.

Even when you marry one and move him to Toronto, he will persistently keep whimpering, "We might move home someday," and secretly be all over PEI real estate on The Google. Trust me on that one.

THINGS TO
DO WHEN
HUMID

Island Cuisine

Island cooking. At one time, it meant boiling the colour out of your meat and vegetables until grey, mashable, and safe for the toothless at the table.

As late as the 1960s, my farmer grandfather rejected even the notion of potato salad. "These potatoes is cold," he stonewalled, pushing the plate back across at his Boston-dwelling daughter. Don't even start with the lettuce. That's for cattle.

These days, the humble PEI potato regularly proves it can clean the soil out of its eyes for a fancy supper. On haute-cuisine menus, it can take a full paragraph to describe the career path that brought a potato from farm to fork.

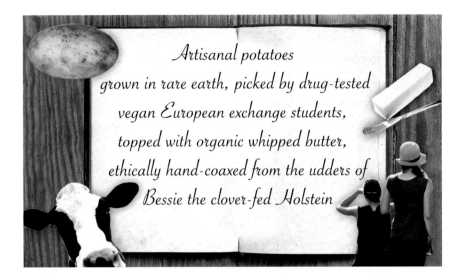

Artisanal potatoes grown in rare earth, picked by drug-tested vegan European exchange students, topped with organic whipped butter, ethically hand-coaxed from the udders of Bessie the clover-fed Holstein

There is more talk devoted to eating local, as well.

Some foodies attempt to eat strictly within a hundred-mile radius. Be warned that by November, all Island fruit available within a hundred miles is actually a turnip. You can carve it into pineapple shapes, if it makes you feels better about your lumpy smoothie.

We know more about our food in these times, which is both blessing and curse. If you're still on the dating scene, here's a thought. Ask yourself this at the end of a first date: "Did I receive more background on the chicken than I did about the date I ate it with?"

There's a point where knowing more about our food risks crossing a line, into grocery shopping at the petting farm.

My strategy is to locate meat that stands at just the right distance away from me. I call it my Goldilocks Zone. I want meat that's not too alien, but also not so up-close-and-familiar that I feel personally culpable. I'm looking for something in between. Just right, like Goldilocks and her porridges.

For example, when the menu enlightens me that the Island pigs were "raised on grass and given sunlight and space to run," that's dancing on the brink of too much information. Were the pigs also told whom they should be running from?

An improved Goldilocks Zone menu option would be "low-salt pulled pork sandwich, featuring pigs from this area code." If you tell me the pig's name was Pinky McDigits, and he knew his numbers up to ten, that sandwich gets infused with the wrong sort of tenderness.

It's not going to be a low-salt sandwich if I end up crying all over it.

Island Camping

I've heard Islanders say, "Camping is in my blood." You can probably get a shot for that health issue, which you likely acquired while camping.

If you trace bloodlines back far enough, you'll always discover ancestors who lacked a hard roof. Most human development happened to avoid camping. Now, in the name of vacation, here you go dragging your family back into the woods, you enemy of history.

Similar to being a nudist or a vegan, a camping lifestyle casts aside the hard-won achievements of your great-grandparents. Let's elect to get damp and undernourished and bet that discomfort will be a trail to heightened appreciation.

Yes, a better appreciation of unclammy pants and safely cooked meat. And this appreciation will hit you, like an unhitched RV, about three hours into camping.

We are not really going to touch RVing. These people will talk to you for two hours straight about the integrity of their septic hookups. And that is why they have to keep moving from place to place.

You'd think that Islanders would be inoculated against further camping by their first experiences. I remember mine, and I'm shocked it's still legal for Canadian Tire to sell tents graded "water-resistant." Have you ever wondered why that evil Scottish Overlord is laughing, on the Canadian Tire money? He is laughing at the thought of you out in the woods in that tent, ye wee shivering and timorous eejit.

It is not a pleasant rite-of-passage to spend a night outside as an eighteen-year-old, shielded only by a K-Way with a couple kite parts. These tents resist water in the way my teen self resisted alcohol. Maybe five minutes of, "No, I really couldn't," followed by several hours of absorbing all liquids in the surrounding area.

A Canadian Tire tent also serves as a take-out container for mosquitoes. You can hear them abuzz with excitement for the convenient delivery of yourself to the woods, just before they pull open the fifteen-cent plastic zipper.

"You should bring citronella candles, or Avon's Skin So Soft," my Mom suggested, to ward off mosquitoes. The mosquitoes seemed to appreciate how the candles and moisturizer helped create the right atmosphere, so they were in the mood to dine and then procreate using my blood.

Some popular Island mosquito repellents

That brings us to why alcohol is the constant companion of camping: "We'll drink this golden forgetting juice, until we can overlook the fact we don't have a house tonight."

When the camping gets rough, the hope is always that conditions will improve. And they will, if you camp and drink for a full seven days.

Mosquitoes regenerate every week. Once the local population has consumed enough of your high-alcohol-percentage blood, they don't do a good job raising the next generation of pupae. The teens get too lazy to bite and just hang around picking at the congealed ketchup stains on your picnic table.

Either that, or at the seven-day point, they're repelled by the smell of your clothes.

You have succeeded at camping, and failed at the last two hundred years of humanity.

Summer Fashion

Island fashion follows the crop cycles of the potato. In winter, we conceal starchy hearts in brown jackets and locate whatever cold storage works. In summer, time to briefly blossom. Expose your unroughened skin to the air and make your tiny stand on Island roadsides.

In winter, when going to the grocery store, it is practical to wear whatever rebuffs wind and any other interest that swirls around you. An outfit pairing sweatpants and a 1991 Canada Winter Games volunteer jacket projects a plucky attitude of community spirit. But summertime means shedding that jacket, probably for good.

If you're trying to make a statement that "I'm playful-yet-grounded," consider something from the PEI Dirt Shirt collection. There are muscle shirts or longer sleeves for the less muscular like me. There're even PEI Dirt Bags, available for pickup near the yacht club.

These bags can be helpful for groceries in winter, if you manage to get them in the store. It's frustrating, though, when you're already in the dairy section, two kilometres diagonal from the entrance, and then remember, "Hey, where is my PEI Dirt Bag?" He's still sitting out in the car, with heat and smart phone running, not helping you with the shopping.

The rusty-downspout colour is created by the iron-y soil of the Island. Your older agricultural relatives will appreciate this irony, of paying good money for a professionally soiled shirt.

When summer comes to historic old Charlottetown, gone are the rustling sounds of abandoned *Guardian* newspapers – the only occupants in February. Our streets transform into boulevards straight out of Montreal, bustling with unrequested jazz.

As you continue up town, you're going to need a switch in handbag. What are fashion experts saying about the handbag of choice for summer on PEI? For the eighth summer running, it's going to be the Sobeys recycled handbag. I mean the classic, with the closeup of a kiwi's crossparts on it.

Some people prefer the fabricky Superstore bags. I find those best for picking up light groceries and every strand of hair from the last three years of my pet's life.

The green Sobeys bags are versatile for all lugging occasions, whether you've got ten pounds of thawing barbecue meat or hand-me-downs to leave in the rain on someone's deck. They are bright, strong, and repellent, especially after carrying the thawing hamburger.

Sobeys bags are also acceptable as checked luggage at the PEI airport, if you duct tape them closed.

HOCKEY AND OTHER STRANGE LOVES

Island Hockey Connections

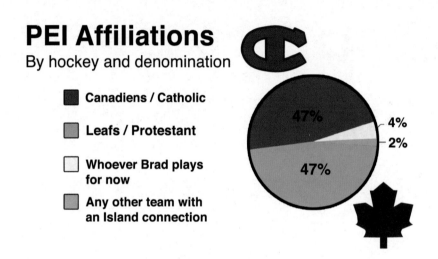

PEI Affiliations
By hockey and denomination

- Canadiens / Catholic
- Leafs / Protestant
- Whoever Brad plays for now
- Any other team with an Island connection

47%

4%

2%

47%

Hockey runs through every starchy molecule of Prince Edward Island.

It's the scent of Zamboni diesel in the rink fries of the society. We can't decide if they're actually made to go together or just a slightly noxious combination we've come to love.

On the Island, you're assigned your hockey team at birth, right at the hospital, with your religion and politics. It might as well be stamped on your PEI identification, beside the organ donor status.

In terms of hockey team denomination, the Island population breaks down pretty much between a Red Team and a Blue Team, like politics and religion. Somewhere around forty-seven per cent Red and forty-seven per cent Blue. Most are pretty dyed-in-the-wool and keep wearing their colours long after they get itchy and could really use a complete airing out.

I was born Canadiens/Catholic. I don't ever remember choosing – it's just always been that way. Ever since I can recall, I've been swearing at the TV on Saturday night and then attending another institution on Sunday morning to ask forgiveness for it.

I had a friend intervene once and ask me why I keep following the Canadiens/Catholic ritual, because "it doesn't seem to make me very happy." What a naïve question. Not all of life is about being happy. This friend now lives in Vancouver, and I am not surprised.

Another almost half of the Island is Leafs/Protestant. I don't follow their same belief system, but I respect them. They're devout through hard times. I sincerely hope that what they believe in happens someday, before or after they die.

A goal light, now and again, must cheer up the life spent in darkness.

Having a Dog

My wife Tara and I have a dog named Viva. That's Spanish, for "unteach-able." Because she doesn't seem to relate to the most basic English words we say around her.

We've had Viva for ten years. She's what's called a rescued dog. My role in this rescue was not ultra heroic – we picked her up at the Humane Society. In fairness, I would not rely on Viva to rescue me either. She would forget me down in a well if there was even a hint of a squirrel heartbeat detectable in the area.

Viva is very smart in ways that have trained us how to behave in our own house. She learned how to open the oven. I wanted to install a wireless security camera, just to see how she did it. Our roast chickens now cool at an altitude, perched atop the fridge.

She was also responsible for the disappearance of our bright pink earplugs off the nightstand, because of their uncanny resemblance to Snausage dog treats.

We've made good-intentioned attempts to train Viva. We purchased DVDs from TV's famous Dog Whisperer, Cesar Millan. I heard Viva laugh when we took them out of the packaging.

Cesar Millan insists that you can become an alpha to your dog through body posture and tone of voice. I'm thinking, every day, Viva watches me follow her around and squat to scoop up her leavings with a grocery bag. A couple of times seeing me in that demeaning posture, and she's figured out I'm not the alpha. "This guy? My alpha? He's my poo butler, from all evidence I can see."

Like many born runners, Viva needed reconstructive knee surgery, during a recent off-season. The poor girl had her hind end shaved clean as a chicken. We took her on rehab walks through snow banks, holding a stomach sling to support her bare haunches.

It was not easy scooping with the bag while holding her in the sling as she tried to leave the still-steaming scene. Several cars slowed, rolled down their windows, and asked if I was having the medical emergency.

The summer after she recovered from surgery, we let Viva off-leash at the dog beach, thinking she would still be picking her runs carefully. But she must have seen something glint 1.7 kilometres away, because off she rocketed down the beach on her line-of-credit bionic knee.

Tara had just settled in on her towel, glistening with cocoa butters. "Go after her," she said, not opening her eyes. I lurched my pointy frame into a sprint after Viva with only a swimsuit to conceal my shrinking self-esteem.

When I caught up with Viva, she had intervened in a family picnic and huffed back two full Subway subs with the cellophane still on them. Two children were crying. I apologized to the family as best I could. All the time, Viva was standing there breathing like a weather windsock, her breath catching on a small piece of Saran Wrap tickling somewhere.

I was concerned. And, I have to admit, part of me was curious as well.

I thought, "Will this all come out pre-bagged?"

And the answer is no. It will come out all over your basement, with a blue knot of Saran Wrap thrown off to the side. I promised Tara, "I'll clean that up." And then she went away for the weekend.

Do you know what a Swiffer won't pick up after you forget about it for 48 hours? For a job like that, you're going to need more than a J-cloth on a curtain rod.

We get pets and expect we'll train them into perfect housemates.

But we've now had almost ten years together, as woman, man, and dog. And I realize that the biggest part of keeping a best friend is forgiving all the things that will never, ever change.

To our sweet Viva, who died January 2015

Islander Day Valentines

Islanders complain that Valentine's Day was invented by Hallmark to sell greeting cards. It's a plausible theory.

So the creation of a second February holiday, called Islander Day, did not arrive as a completely welcome announcement. Sure, what more fitting tribute to things PEI than a day off work? On the third Monday in February, many of us are unscheduled to start with, but that's quibbling.

What's difficult about the new holiday is finding Islander Day cards suited to the occasion.

Given the unresponsiveness of the North American greetings industry to Island needs, I've developed a set of specialty cards combining Valentine's Day and Islander Day.

These Islander Valentines are ideal, because they can arrive any time between February fourteenth and the third Monday in February. All our mail is now getting routed through Halifax, as if it needs to see a vascular surgeon or something. So this doubling-up keeps your belated bases covered.

These Islander Valentine cards speak love Island-style, like wearing pants from Mark's Work Wearhouse on a date. Pleated enough for romance, yet anchored in the fleecy comfort of home.

How about an Islander Valentine that's potato-shaped?

You're my dear sweet Russet Burbank

Pretty rough and even dirty before peeled.

Under that, you've got the cleanest of hearts

And you scrub up pretty good before meals.

Here's another Islander Valentine that plays with the tantalizing shape of the Island itself, entitled "Bikini Brief."

The Island can be a discouraging place for singles looking for love. Everyone knows everyone, and it's hard to ask someone discreetly about their status.

So my final Island Valentine is a functional questionnaire, intended to determine if the recipient is emotionally available.

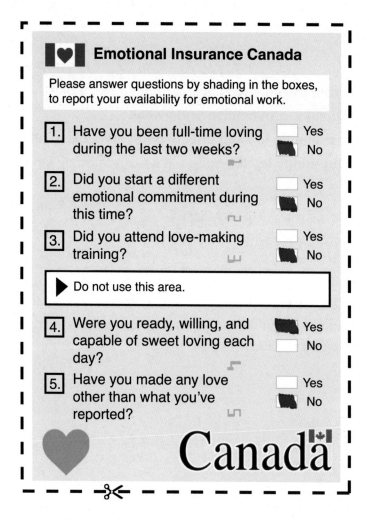

GETTING OVER THE BRIDGE

The Confederation Bridge between Prince Edward Island and New Brunswick is the longest bridge over ice-covered waters in the world. There may be longer bridges. But those cross over aquamarine, pee-warm waters dancing with tropical fish, and what's the challenge in constructing those?

The Confederation Bridge opened in 1997 to worldwide fanfare. But nobody on the Island is that excited about it anymore.

The Bridge has become just another part of the landscape, a twelve-storey high Tim Horton's drive-thru. Neither Tim's coffee nor the Bridge is that great, but they're both necessary for getting through New Brunswick.

The old marketing slogan for the Bridge was "Get Over It." And it seems we have.

I think it's high time for some new marketing, to re-excite people on both sides of the Northumberland Strait.

How about unearthing the Island's anxiety complex about getting hooked up to the mainland? That unease gave the crossing a real burn.

Previous to being named for Confederation, the bridge was popularly known as the Fixed Link.

If you heard that your dog was getting fixed, what would you think? That the dog had an operation and lost something identity-based in the bargain. We want the marketing to unleash that fear about the Bridge, and meet it straight on.

PEI is fixed.
But we're nobody's
little Shihtzu.

Many Islanders were originally against the Bridge because they thought it would allow more unwanted substances into the province. You see, Moncton drug-dealers were too bashful to take a ferry.

These fears haven't really proven substantial. Nowadays, the only law-related sign around the Bridge indicates that it is illegal to import honeybees. I don't even know how to tell an off-Island bee from a local one.

Maybe our marketing could play with this edge. The ads could suggest that the Bridge serves as a tempting Gateway Village that leads inevitably to even more intoxicating villages within our Island.

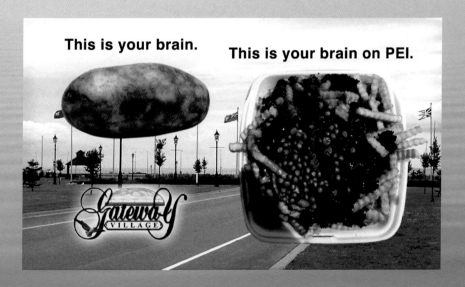

Science has shown that it takes fifty years for "fries with the works" to exit your system. Every minute is worth it.

Not sure how mild-mannered Islanders might feel about our tourism marketing entering this danger zone? All I'm saying is that with the Confederation Bridge, the edge is already there, staring you in the face.

If you picture the Northumberland Strait as a blue bedspread, what is the conspicuous bulge rising out of the middle of the Bridge? A touch of subliminal advertising might do the trick.

The engineers claim that the Bridge has a slight curve and rise to keep drivers alert. Looks like we've got somebody's attention.

Let's face some basic facts about the Bridge. Nobody likes paying to get off.

The tolls have converted PEI into the hotel mini-bar of provinces. We don't charge anything for people on the way over, as if to shout, "Hey, we're tasty and fun-sized. Enjoy the hospitality." And then guests get dinged with a huge bill when they try to check out.

We need to spin it so that the visitor has a choice, where not paying the forty-five dollar toll could be a down payment on the future.

It could be the next plank in an Island repopulation initiative, providing us with the boost we need.

GETTING SCHOOLED

The Debate: Is the e-Book Superior to the Old-Fashioned Paper Book?

My answer: Yes, it is.

For starters, print books smell weird, like a shut-in relative.

Even new books arrive in a dust jacket. Think about that word. It tells you that dust is the main thing that's going to be picked up, now this depressing paperweight has entered your life.

I can already hear your romantic eulogies for holding a book. I recall that physical experience with a tinge of disgust. Oh, the thrill of opening a library book and being involuntarily entered into a game of "Name that Stain." I hope whatever is on page forty-seven is chocolate.

With a wifi-enabled e-reader, I can instantly connect what I'm reading to the best that has been known and thought in all human history. No more inconvenient footnotes, squirrelled away at the back of a ball-breaking Shakespeare anthology.

Now when I'm on my e-reader, and I read an unfamiliar line in *Romeo and Juliet*, like "on the prick of noon," I just Google it. And believe you me, I'll never unlearn what I saw.

I'm in a Men's Book Club. Give your brain a second to adjust to that non sequitur. Most of the men have switched to e-readers, and that's a major relief. Our sessions used to be full of rambly so-called book comments from guys who can't keep their inner child in the car seat.

Now, we eat up most of our meeting time comparing e-reader features. The air is heavy with interesting perspectives, such as, "Yes, mine is shorter and thicker, but I like how the extra weight feels in my hands."

Another positive is that you can change the text size with e-readers. That's a plus for older members of my Men's Book Club. I think iPads should be required for reading as soon as you hit forty, automatic as a prostate exam. You can learn so much, using just one finger.

E-books expose that all reading is basically non-forever. It's e-phemeral, maybe smarter than *etalk*, but no more lasting. Reading is Ben Mulroney applying hairspray. It clouds the head briefly and then evaporates into pure nothingness.

Life of Pi changed your life? Name one specific thing you remember from that book. "I think there's a big tiger in it?" I thought so. That thirty hours of your life has now disappeared out to sea.

Finally, as an author, I have lived the comparison between print books and e-books. Every time I go down to the basement, I have to trip over stacked, unsold boxes of my first collection.

I also issued the book for e-reader, and it was downloaded no fewer than a dozen times. I never have to look at the millions of unsold e-book copies. They evaporate, as silent and secret as my unspoken hopes.

School Supplies

The back-to-school flyers return every fall, pushing what's necessary for students to succeed. Used to be, all I needed was a new set of pencil crayons in the kitbag. Sharpen my Laurentiens, and colour me good to go.

I kept my pencils in a monogrammed pencil case I crafted myself in Home Economics class. I ran out of time on the assignment and had to staple the last two sides of that puppy closed. It rusted, but it lasted. I'm thankful to have acquired this essential job skill of fashioning a holder for my pencils.

In junior high, one place I took all my HB pencils, was to the guidance counsellor's office for a career aptitude test. I filled in the question circles pertaining to my interests. "Do you like throw pillows, or do you prefer the smell of diesel?"

When I was finished, a computer ran an analysis of my answers and printed out a list of suggested careers on dot-matrix paper where you have to rip the holes off the sides. I remember all of my suggested careers involved working with animals, alone. Veterinarian. Taxidermist.

My plan, coming out of junior high school, was to open PEI's first veterinarian-taxidermist operation. I had the marketing all figured out.

One fall in middle school, the parents splurged for my new back-to-school K-Way. I loved that K-Way. I kept wearing it well into December, waiting for the bus in frigid rural PEI. Windbreaker, my arse.

Once I arrived at school, the K-Way folded up into its own belted pocket. That pocket was not for pencils and pens. Those went into the pencil case. The packet was for your fingers and ears, which had frozen and fallen off while you were out waiting for the bus in December, in a K-Way.

Today's back-to-school flyers make me wistful for the late 1980s. It was a more innocent time, when teens used words like "wistful."

According to the flyers, a new iPad is now essential for a junior high student.

Back in the day, it took more imagination to use screen-based technology. I learned to flip my solar-powered calculator around and write the word "h3LL0," with upside-down numbers. Hello, is it me you're looking for? Lionel Richie probably discovered this as he was dancing on the ceiling, looking at someone else's calculator.

I mastered this calculator writing trick and wrote "h3LL0" to the girl sitting beside me in home room. I also could write "B00BL3SS." Which I kept to myself, because I noticed that word was the opposite of what happened to her that summer.

In middle school in the 1980s, determining if someone liked me seemed to have higher stakes. What is her status? Not easily available pre-social networks.

I spent two hours with a Magic 8-Ball, trying to trace a statistical pattern in yes-no questions regarding her liking me. "Concentrate and ask again," commanded the Magic 8-Ball. Not good for the self-esteem, having my attention deficits diagnosed by a paperweight.

Teens today waste too much time online. I learned about focus and concentration, with my Magic 8-Ball in the TV room watching multiple episodes of *The Facts of Life.* "Will I date someone blonde and sophisticated like Blair, or a no-nonsense brunette like Jo?" Reply hazy, try again.

It was risky to make friends in middle school, more difficult than a simple finger-click on a notification. Making 500 friends? Impossible.

To put a message out there to a possible friend, I needed to write a tiny note on looseleaf with a pen and then remove the ink and springs from that same pen. Then roll the note inside the casing, reassemble the pen, and hope other classmates would baton-pass it to the intended recipient without intercepting it themselves. Making friends via this PaperMate social network was as time-consuming as prison contraband.

No wonder I only had three friends. I only had three pens.

The Debate: Should University Be Free to All Who Wish to Attend?

My answer: Oui.

"Man is born free and everywhere he is chains." That's Jean-Jacques Rousseau, French philosopher.

The tuition-cost of me learning that quote: $20,000. Books and residence: $15,000. Finding out how much the world actually values my Bachelor of Arts: priceless.

Education is a right, and it should flow as freely and constantly as a public library urinal.

University used to be only for the idle rich, a finishing school for the handing down of Latin and man-spankings. Now, universities are critical economic engines, responsible for producing ninety-five per cent of Canada's statistics about the importance of universities.

But the chains of high tuition are locking those doors once more.

And for what? To maintain privilege. University professors are over-paid. There are better ways of subsidizing Canada's sales of corduroy blazers and European hatchbacks.

I'm impressed by developments like the Quebec student strikes. I wanted to bang pots and pans in solidarity – "Give us Kraft dinner, or give us death."

Because I know my debt-fuelled bachelor's degree sentenced me to a decade living in bachelor apartments. My mattress reeked of pasta cooked only five feet away.

What's the real economic value of a university degree anymore? Look at the ratio in your average first-year psychology class. Three-hundred young people, all staring at one bearded fifty-year-old. That's the exact opposite of age ratios in Internet dating.

Neither is a healthy scenario. I don't need a psychology degree to tell you that.

Our society treats learning opposite to the way we treat love. We say, you *have* to pay for it, or it's not legitimate. Put an economics professor on a street corner and see how many cars pull up to buy a drink from his wisdom cup. That's called the free market.

I think it's perfectly okay for a young person to spend a couple of years pursuing a Major in Self-Esteem, with a Minor in Realistic Expectations. I did. But let's allow them to take this trip without picking up a future-sucking debt tapeworm.

Here in Canada, a half-million student loan recipients recently learned that the federal government lost a hard drive with their personal details, opening them to identity theft.

I graduated with two English degrees and $25,000 in debt. Go ahead and steal that identity.

Hope you have more luck making money from it than I did.

PEI Economic Breakdown

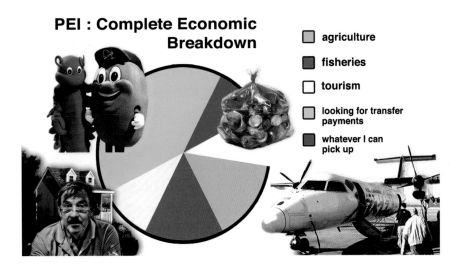

PEI : Complete Economic Breakdown

- ⬜ agriculture
- ⬛ fisheries
- ⬜ tourism
- ⬜ looking for transfer payments
- ⬛ whatever I can pick up

If it were a chair, the Island economy would be on three legs.

These legs would be, of course, the agriculture, the fishery, and the tourism. The agriculture and the fishery have certain challenges. Our Island population cannot eat the full bounty of the land and sea, although we try our damnedest. We need to create export markets, and that is easier said than done.

Look at the lobster and potato mascots that we send to international trade shows. The lobster and the potato are two of the most challenging organisms to make into lovable mascots. One resembles a space spider, more likely to burst from your stomach than go gently into it. The other resembles a bumpy, brown cloud. Both risk scaring off children and investments.

The tourism is also a risky industry, where we bet our livelihoods on how a Bostonian's brain will react to variability in the Weather Channel and Middle East oil prices. Once, tourism was as simple as renting out the bedroom of the adult child you're not on speaking terms with. Those days are gone.

A growing industry on the Island is looking for transfer payments. So much fun. The tiny plane from Charlottetown to Ottawa is like a tin can full of springy snakes, disguised as peanuts. Everyone from the caucus to the cockpit laughing, swapping tips on how to ask for transfers. Is it okay to suggest a transfer when you're meeting someone in Ottawa for the first time? Yes, but you should probably buy dinner.

Back on Island soil, the "whatever I can pick up" sector continues to expand. Helping that guy with a truckload, pet grooming and/or breeding, cleaning of unlocked car interiors. I'm personally in this sector. I'll perform at your fundraiser for a dinner plate, fix your dampened iPhone, and sort out what's worth anything in those blue bags. When November comes to PEI, you have to do more than one thing.

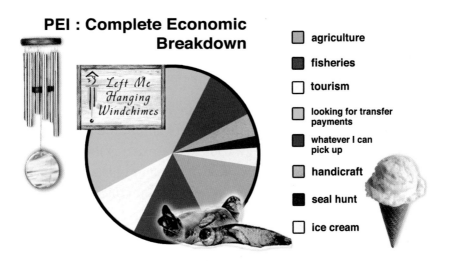

PEI : Complete Economic Breakdown

- agriculture
- fisheries
- tourism
- looking for transfer payments
- whatever I can pick up
- handicraft
- seal hunt
- ice cream

Left Me Hanging Windchimes

The remaining economic activity on PEI is a potpourri made up of handicraft, seal hunts, and ice cream.

There is limitless room for growth in handicraft, because the crafts are unrelated to any actual need that could be filled. If you're willing to shell out $75 for a set of wind chimes to tell you that it's windy on PEI, you have a good amount of disposable income.

Handicrafts always tell a story. Sometimes, the story of why someone fled civilization and came to PEI to open a playfully titled handicraft business. Broken Promises Stained Glass. Left Me Hanging Windchimes.

Don't worry, no seals are harmed in the making of the PEI seal industry. We're focused on hitting up the occasional celebrity for helicopter-and-penthouse-hotel rentals when they come to watch the seals not get hunted, from the air. The only club is mile-high.

And finally, ice cream. Is there anything more delectable? Island scientists have been expanding the industry far beyond plain vanilla, with value-added biotechnology. Look at real existing flavours such as "Island Fantasy." Scientists distilled the dreams of Islanders into a coagulant, and then pressi-jetted that straight into the ice cream.

Island Fantasy is an Alpine beer sorbet, with a faint tobacco ripple, all on a scratch-n-win cone. With an ice cream like that, I'm set for life.

THROUGH
THE BABY
GATES

The Debate: Is it Wrong to Pick a Baby Name That Is Strange, Exotic, or Made Up?

My answer: No, unusual names are great.

My name is Patrick. You may recognize my name from such long-running television ads as, "It's Patrick, and he bought life insurance."

I would pay good money to have a name so strange it would never be featured in such ads. No, *this* Patrick did not buy life insurance. I'm a self-employed comedian in Canada's smallest province. On a good day, my life insurance plan is Optimum points.

What does a traditional name like "Patrick" tell you about me as an individual? The name comes laden with a history of Catholic guilt and rhythm-method resentments. I grew up in a house so Catholic, I still can't say the words "pull-out couch" without blushing.

My wife had a delightful made-up name for her first few days. *Shirlene.* The name rings with a sheen of modernity, or at least the earthy-toned seventies version of it. Then, her mother's best friend intervened and said, "What are you thinking?" The already-born girl was renamed with the more conventional "Tara."

I love who Tara became. But in that moment, our society was robbed of a sassy waitress named Shirlene, perfumed with polyester, menthol, and burnt toast. Those waitresses are rare now, and, as any red-blooded man will tell you, they are unforgettable.

I think the baby names of this new millennium should be like brands of bottled water. Google-friendly and aggressively ignorant toward history.

Don't cast for baby names in the dried-up riverbed of your relatives' hopes. Name your children for fictional wellsprings that spout 100 per cent dreams. Evian! Dasani! Aquafina! Climb in the back seat of this all-wheel drive Denali. We're headed to the box mart to tear open a twenty-four-pack of the future.

We laugh at news items about parents legally prevented from naming a baby "Nutella." What's wrong with branding your child as distinctively sweet and nutty? If one or two schoolkids have a punchy reaction to that, they should be made to go eat lunch in another room.

My elementary school roll-call in the eighties sounded like a self-help meeting, because everyone needed a last initial to differentiate them from identically named kids. David M., Jennifer S., Chris D.

These people grew up and, in today's digital world, now need to invent exotic names for themselves, because jen@gmail.com is always taken. When I see the awful usernames they come up with, even for work, I wonder how could their parents have done worse?

When I was teaching college, I had students applying to the program via email. One potential student jotted off an application from the username flamingnipples19@hotmail.com. No other name attached. As a professional educator, how am I supposed to reply to this expression of interest?

"Dear flamingnipples19 – I regret to inform that your lack of experience, and teats of absolute fire, make you a poor fit for our program. Maybe look to join another group, with others who share the same disorder. As there appear to be at least 18 others out there."

Exotic names are the new normal, in this creative economy. It's not enough to name your child Kesha. Make that "s" into a money symbol, if you want her to be searchable on YouTube.

Our toddler is named Nathaniel. When he's not getting the attention he deserves at daycare, we demand that an umlaut consistently appear over the "i." Nathanïel. If that doesn't change things, the final "e" and "l" in his name will convert into the symbols for the Euro and the British pound. Nathanï€£. We have planned for his future.

Exotic names possess a magical power, as the fairy tale Rumpelstiltskin reminds us. It's the story of a mischievous elf who gains the right to inherit a mother's first-born unless the mother can guess the elf's weird name. Rumpelstiltskin.

Everybody glosses over a guessable name like Patrick. All it tells you is that I'm Catholic and old enough that I probably had my Rumpelstiltskin removed after birth without anyone asking me.

Name-wise, I say err on the side of leaving baby with a touch too much. If something is too frou-frou and gets in his way, it can always be trimmed back when he's an adult and can choose for himself.

In closing, consider the moral of the classic Johnny Cash song, "A Boy Named Sue." It is this: you should pre-emptively shatter your child's chance at peace by giving him or her a weird name. She will then build up scar tissue, by repeatedly walking over shattered illusions about the goodness of people.

Your child will grow up to thank you. Or at the very least, you can have a nice cathartic bar fight, once little man Sue finally hunts you down.

Zen and the Art of Baby Maintenance

When our son was born, we were given a book called *What to Expect from Your Newborn*. It has 800 pages. He didn't read a single one of them.

After several years, I've learned more lessons from our little grasshopper than I've taught him. These lessons have pushed my expectations aside and cast me into a more Zen-like attitude.

Nothing brings one into the moment more vividly than waking at 3:00 AM to glimpse a brown stain just cresting the neckline of a onesie. That is the living present, which must be encountered.

How can companies sell diapers labelled "eighteen to twenty-eight pounds" when they do not hold even close to that poundage? Is anything that poops up its own neck fully human? These are good questions, but for another time.

Here are some other important Zen lessons my baby son has taught me.

STRENGTH OF EGO

My wife Tara has a book called *The Power of Now*. I've cracked it open and plan on reading the whole thing a bit later. I've gleaned kernels of wisdom along the lines of this: The main cause of unhappiness is never the situation but your thoughts about it. Deep matters.

My son does not accept this radical responsibility as an individual. He embraces "The Power of No." This one-word worldview deems the situation to be unacceptable, and his own thoughts about it to be 100 per cent superfine, thank you very much. No, no, no. It makes his ego into a shiny unscalable fortress.

The situation? Going out of the house in February wearing snowpants. His thoughts about it? No. No pants, one rubber boot, and a dragon cape.

I'm starting to see the strength of his philosophy. Last week, I answered forty emails in an hour and just typed "No" to all of them. My inbox is empty. Nothing reaches the tower of my soul.

DETACHMENT FROM MATERIAL THINGS

My wife and I are not *Home and Garden* material, but our house had acquired an off-the-rack yogapant chic. Our friends warned us to start baby-proofing six months before arrival. Stock up on foam corners and plugs until the house is as neutered as a bouncy castle.

Two years in, I know baby-proofing is impossible.

What you should do is to detach from your material possessions. Baby is going to lead you to this mindset eventually, by smashing most of them. I suggest starting this journey six months before, by pre-emptively destroying your favourite possessions. Do it yourself. At least you'll have some control and a proper chance to say goodbye.

Goodbye flat-screen TV. I'm going to cut your cables with safety scissors and then run the blades across your plasma. I'm going to lick peanut butter into the front of your remote, until you won't play anything but *A & E*. Because I accept that's how it's going to be now.

I've become so detached from things, I no longer link the state of our home with my personal sense of worth. That would be crushing.

HEALTH AND HUMILITY

Having our son means that we meditate carefully on food and what enters into our little nature's miracle.

His blended fruits and vegetables arrive in packets from an organic planet. The packaging announces exotic contents like Kiwi, Quinoa, Kale, and Mangosteen.

I do not know what these are, but they sound positive. I couldn't be happier with these packets if they contained salagadoola and mechicka boola, with enriched bibbidi-bobbidi-boo.

Their pricing is similar to buying rounds of piña colada on an airplane.

So when our son spits out a mouthful of the fruit mash, I eat it off his tray, as a way of conserving this value. It's a move that I call the reverse baby bird. Rather than the parent robin chewing up the food for the hatchling, it's the other way around.

And so it is said, we must think again with the child's mind, to truly enter the kingdom of awareness.

Nate, summer 2013

The Debate: Are Grandparents a Bad Influence on the Grandkids?

My answer: Yes, they are.

Grandparents treat children like car rentals: "Oh, here's a fun little number I don't own." They whip them around, cover them in candy-wrappers, and then dump them back at your door, overheated. "You clean this unit up."

We have a two-year-old son. I told his grandmother, "Watch the sugar." And then came back a couple hours later to discover he'd had two bowls of jujubes in lieu of dinner. Why did you give him those? "Well, he wanted them." Is that a good reason to get him so pumped full of bright, plasticky sugar he comes home and poops Kindertoys for the next week?

Besides, since when are you in the business of giving little boys what they want, Iron Lady? I asked you for a Joe Louis cake for six straight years and never tasted a single crumb of one.

Grandparent babysitting is not free. It's powered by passive-aggressive energy.

Everything we do with baby gets covered in a shiny layer of guilt. "The waste of these disposables. I hand-laundered every one of your diapers and never saw a rash on you." Well, all hail to you, Queen of the Behinds.

I would happily pay a teenage girl ten dollars an hour to sit in my house and not judge me. That came out sounding terrible, but you know what I mean.

We drop our son off at the grandparents' for a little babysitting and arrive back to some scene of half-dressed havoc. "Just airing him out," says Grandma.

Our son knows how to turn on Netflix, and Grandma doesn't, so even at her own place, she gives him the controller. But the two-year-old can't get it to "Kids" setting, and he sits in front of three continuous hours of her *Downton Abbey*, naked. Now all he wants to wear is a top hat and a monocle and no pants. He's turning into Mr. Peanut.

Grandparents are a bad influence, because they're regressing in every key area where we want our kids to progress.

We're working on language with our son. "Don't point and fuss. Use your words." And there's Grandma at Sunday dinner, pointing and saying, "Pass me the thing ... uh ...t he thing with all the little white stuff in it for the top of the food." Mom, use your words.

Our son's teeth are almost all in. We're teaching him to brush and care for them.

Grandma took her teeth out and let the boy play with them, outside on the deck. Then a crow swooped down and stole them, for real.

Eastern Canadian readers, if a crow flashes you a toothy grin in the next year please message me.

If PEI Ruled the World: Maritime Windas

If PEI ruled the world, computers would have operating systems that run at our processing speed. Your system would come with Maritime Windas pre-installed, and not the updated variety.

When you start work in the morning, sometimes Maritime Windas opens up, and sometimes it heaves and gets jammed halfways. When that happens, try again in a couple of days once the pressure settles. No sense trying to move heaven and earth.

With Maritime Windas, tasks will launch and processes will complete, all in good time. You want to try to pin down an exact day and moment when? That reeks of arrogance, to say the least, considering the possible fluctuations in climate, system health, and my actual desire to finish the task.

In defense of the Maritimes, look at the failure of the powerful Microsoft Windows to accurately estimate the time involved in any working process. Today's personal computers have enough compu- tational resources to slingshot Neil Armstrong to the moon several times. But all bets on accuracy are off, once these same computers begin guessing how long it will take to copy vacation pictures to a USB key to print them off at the Shoppers Drug Mart.

When will that folder full of JPEG pictures be fully across? The system churns away with the progress bar and Windows has to revise its esti- mates several times. Probably fifteen minutes – okay, more like thirty seconds – and then, oh hey, my bad, it'll now be two days. All of these self-cancelling guesses do nothing but undermine my confidence. You have no idea where we are on this mission, do you Microsoft?

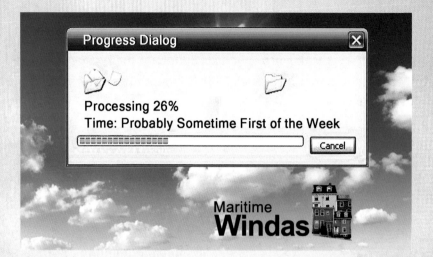

With the Maritime Windas operating system, we learned long ago not to make any big-headed promises about time and exactness.

Ask a Maritimer when any task in progress is going to be complete, such as retrieving necessary paperwork or installing a new set of windows. We will say something more modest and respectful like, "Should be done probably sometime first of the week." The first of which week in particular? Who is to say? Nobody died and made us boss of the entire planet.

Some users newly logged into the Maritime Windas operating system get frustrated with this holistic approach to time. Why don't you get with a more modern system, they object.

Because being up to date presents nothing but a brand new set of unknowns. A new service pack can take out things that were working just fine before, thank you very much. Suddenly, the system can't tell your 1992 dot-matrix printer or 1988 Plymouth Reliant K from a hole in the ground.

Let mainland futurists buy fresh-off-the-lot. We'll wait across the next two decades or so and see if there are any manufacturer's recalls and then have a think about installing.

So when we see that constant dialogue pop up about the Maritimes requiring updates, we just shut it all down.

Because Houston, there's no problem down here. All systems: pretty much fine as they are.

WORD TO MY HOMIES

Home Wreck-novation

As a society, why are we susceptible to the message that we should spend weekends destroying our homes?

Handy Man Special
4 bdrm home,
acre lot, garage, stor-
age bldg. A Steal at
$39,900

Actual Island real estate advertisement.

In PEI real estate ads, even a broke-down farmhouse gets fluffed up as a "handyman's special." These real estate agents should write personals for hard-to-date men: "This bachelor is a 'Self-Sufficient Woman Special.' Do you have a limitless supply of patience, and enough income for two? Well, here's a lifelong project for you." Good luck getting this one to stay standing up.

I worked half my life to partially own a house, with my wife, on paper. Now I'm supposed to spend the next half tearing it apart. And then to go buy more stuff to spackle over what I just made worse with the first load of stuff I bought.

I know I'm no born handyman.

I have six years of post-secondary education in English literature. I can mend a split infinitive or cinch up a dangling participle like nobody's business. But that education hasn't furnished me with the skills to find the right aisle at Home Depot.

Home Depot is overkill for my hardware needs. The whole point of that football-field-sized store is to make me feel inadequate, so I'll buy things rather than ask questions. If the hardware industry wanted me to ask questions comfortably, they would have renamed caulk a long time ago.

So I wander the endless store and see how activities once reserved for trained professionals are repackaged as fun little weekend hobbies. Do-it-yourself kits such as "Pour and Bake a Septic Tank" and "Electrocute Your Way to a Recessed Lighting System."

Why should these tasks be tackled on a holiday Monday by a hungover English major who reads too much into the directions? Hey, there are tense shifts throughout this fine Mandarin translation. I scribble "vague" and "awkward construction" in the margins with a red pen.

On a holiday Monday, all the actual plumbers and electricians are at home, resting on their couches, and not pretending that they know how to do other people's jobs. That's why tradespeople's pants fall down. Because they laugh their arses off at the job you did, before you broke down and called them.

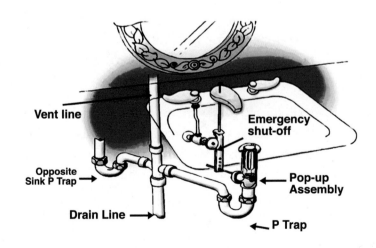

I approach home repair like home health. I don't want to be running off to the professionals in a panic for situations that just require a cough drop or a Band-Aid.

But converting professions into hobbies is a slippery slope. With the medical wait times in Atlantic Canada, and the Home Depot's endless need to expand, how long is it before we see starter kits for simple day surgeries on their shelves?

In weekend nightmares, I hear the phone calls that will happen should these do-it-yourself trends continue .

"Hey Bobby, you know how you stoppered your own tap, to keep more kids from running all over? Getting around to my plumbing. Well, the diagram is from the side, and I'm coming at it more from the top view."

"Is it the blue one or the red one?"

Stud finder or no, there's certain territory I just shouldn't drill into. Stop me if I try.

Chicken Wings for the Soul

I try to live according to values. Little statements I carry to help me through the world. Like grocery coupons, I don't always remember to use them. But I feel better for having put them in my pocket.

I try to buy meat locally, for example. Because of a couple of carried-around values, such as "*Support local poultry*," or "*It's good living in a small community.*"

So on a hectic day this year, on my way to a meeting, I get a text from my wife asking me to pick up chicken wings for unplanned dinner guests. The text says "chicken wigs," but I realize the difference. All chickens I've met have been bald and fairly accepting of it.

I think, "*Support local poultry*" and detour across town to the local meat market, where everybody knows your name. I also do this because I want to (value statement) "*Try to adapt to change.*" My wife texts me small changes of direction though the day to put this value to the test.

Chicken Wings for the Soul

Just as I'm pulling in to the meat market, my cellphone rings with a work-related call. I take the call, because I want to (value statement) *"Keep up a professional appearance."* You know the cellphone pretend-you-are-at-a-desk voice? The other person asks, "Am I getting you at a good time?" and I say "Oh. Never better, fire away," while I take notes on a crumpled napkin, writing with ketchup packets, in my 2001 Pontiac Grand Am. Yes, the name of my vehicle is Grand Ma, with two letters switched. That's how I roll.

I peel into the market parking lot, stop the car, and take the ten-minute phone call. By the time it ends, I'm late for the meeting. So I lock the car and fly like a bird of prey into the market to grasp the chicken wings in my talons. I come running back out and go to unlock the car door. There are my keys in the ignition.

I got distracted during the cell call and locked them in there good and tight. Now I'm left here, holding a big bag of chicken. You got it, Pontiac. Am grand, am late.

I think (another value statement), *"Don't be afraid to ask for help."* What I should do is go back into the market, where everybody knows your name, and ask them to hold my bag of chicken until I can return. They will laugh at me, though, for a period not less than two years.

Then, it dawns on me that my mother lives ten blocks away, and I can sprint up there with my long legs and borrow her tiny Hyundai. Still, I don't want to be seen sprinting ten blocks up the sidewalk in the broad light of day, in a small community, swinging a big bag full of meat. Someone will remark to me in days coming, "Saw you running with a bag of chicken." That's not a *professional appearance.*

"Try to adapt to change." Here's the revised plan. No one's looking. I take the bag full of chicken and safely stow it under the rear tire of the Pontiac. I even walk the perimeter of the car, briefly pretending to be someone else, to determine if I can see the chicken bag, and I don't.

So I run the ten blocks and retrieve Mom's tiny Hyundai. I then ride in self-congratulatory triumph back to the market and look under the rear tire for my hidden cache of meat.

And the bag of chicken is gone. Son of a chicken biscuit. I think, "What kind of person swipes someone else's bag of chicken from beneath the rear tire of a Pontiac?" I try to reflect on *the value of living in a small community. Be bigger than this.*

I decide someone must have needed the chicken worse than I did. I retreat in my mom's Hyundai, completely chicken-less, to make my meeting. It turns out the meeting was changed to another day, by an email that came in during that earlier cellphone call which started the whole problem. "*Try to adapt to change.*"

So it's a week later.

I'm living my values and still shopping for local meat at the same market. I get to chatting with the butcher behind the counter. During a lapse in conscious thinking, I thread into the conversation, "You have many problems with meat theft?" Because I'm still *keeping up the professional appearances*, you understand.

The butcher pauses for a second and asks, "Do you mean from in the store, or ... why do you ask?" And scrambling to remain very nonchalant, I say, "Oh, nothing in particular." He looks at me a long moment and then starts cackling like a freshly foxed henhouse.

When he regains his normal breathing, he tells me the story.

The week before, a senior burst back into the market from the parking lot because she couldn't get into her car. She *wasn't afraid to ask for help*.

There was a horrible Nature Channel scene underway outside. A flock of seagulls was locked in epic bloodsport under a Pontiac Grand Am, fighting to the death for a bag of chicken.

The market sent their new guy out there to retrieve the chicken bag, and he got all pecked to hell so the senior could get into her car. He really had to fight to *keep up professional appearances*. They tried to see who owned the Pontiac, but the keys were locked in the ignition. They wondered who under the sky could have set this havoc in motion.

The butcher perks an eyebrow. "And you're the Birdman."

In my defense, I was simply trying to live my values.

I just didn't think I would be doing it by feeding a chicken picnic to cannibalistic seagulls.

The Debate: Is Making a Phone Call Better Than Sending a Text?

My answer: Yes, phone better. IMHO, texting not gr8.

Call me old-fashioned. I mean, call me on a phone.

I can remember my first time witnessing a good friend constantly text. It was in Europe, where innovations arrive sooner, except for decaf and deodorant.

Our café conversation got interrupted fifteen times as he answered incoming texts. I can remember thinking, "This is rude, even for Europe."

How would you feel if you were having lunch with someone, and they interrupted to accept fifteen meaningless tiny phone calls?

(ring) "Sup?" (click) (ring) "No way!" (click) (ring) "LOL" (click) (ring) "There in a sec." (click) (ring) "Still here with this idiot." (click).

You would stand up and gently punch them in the softest part of the skull.

Texting represents the lowest amount of effort possible for any channel of communication. Even butt-dialling requires that you sit down.

The phone is rich in tone. When a friend calls with bad news, like "I lost my job," you can fake a world of empathy, with just the tone of your voice. When a friend texts about being fired, and you send back a cat emoji, what does that even mean? "Here's a pet to comfort you?" Or "Here begins your descent into becoming a cat person, friendless and smelling of urine."

I phone my wife whenever I can. Because when I text her, tone is a disaster. Everything comes across as Nazi-shouty and dictatorial. Her: "Feeling sick. Pick up chicken vings." Me: "OK, I vill."

I try to soften things up, by tagging "hon" onto my texts with her. And autocorrect substitutes in the man's name "Jon," every single time.

My texts with her read like a fictional three-way with Jon Bon Jovi. "Oh, I'm halfway there, Jon." Curse you, autocorrect. Once I sent, "You still feel suck, Jon?"

She texted back, "You are an ash-hat." At least there was no mistaking her tone.

Calling someone on the phone means one thing to me: commitment. I know what that word means to millennials. Commitment means "cellular plan" and "how to get out of."

But because I grew up with the phone, I learned about commitment. When I was seventeen, and someone made me tingly in my tender parts, here's what I needed to do, to ask her on a date.

For my eight-person family, we had one rotary-dial phone, bolted to the kitchen wall. My parents opted for an additional feature – a longer stretchy cord.

If I had feelings for someone, I needed to dial seven digits on that rotary dial and wait as each number rotated back, an agonizing pause where the sparks of my courage could die.

I needed to stretch the cord to the maximum to get behind the basement door. Before any hope of reaching my beloved, I needed to first speak to her father, who answered.

If you're seventeen today and want to hook up, you fire off a text before the synapse has fully fired in your brain. "Sup, girl." And if she hasn't responded in seven seconds, you're texting a JPEG of your junk to somebody else.

Is that the kind of world you want to live in? Sign me up for the phone plan, with the long-term commitment.

THINGS TO DO WHEN FREEZING

Islander Winter Activities

Island winter is long and difficult. It gets worse in February, when other Islanders start asking if I'm going South this year. This question usually means two things: Yes, the asker is going South, and no, I am not.

I have enough Air Miles for tropical punch drink boxes. Stick a straw in my Tetra Pak this February, looks like I'll be sucking it up.

Besides, if I went South, I'd miss out on all my favourite wintertude goings-on. Here are four ways to make your own fun in an Island winter, whether as a family or all by yourself.

FENDERBERG KICK-OFF

PEI is famous for the largest fenderbergs east of Montreal. A fenderberg is the snowpack buildup found under car tire rims. The Island's slushy temperatures and Islanders' let-it-hang attitude toward cars make for ideal fenderberg-growing conditions. Take the family on a fun-hunt through town, challenging each other to find and kick off the Titanic of all fenderbergs. Don't try and tell me that's not satisfying.

BOBSLED TRAINING

The Island has produced more than its fair share of Olympic gold-medal bobsledders, despite lacking a bobsled track. The reason? Island secondary roads. All winter, they're a province-wide sledding track, with only a scatter of sand to suggest where the next turn could be. These roads are a breeding ground for steely-nerved people with huge calves from pushing family sedans out of ditches.

BLACK ICE BREAKDANCING

You know what this is: you step on black ice and catch yourself in a three-second uprock routine, arms and legs popping. Nothing makes a heart skip faster. Except maybe sticking around to watch someone else do it next.

ALPINE CLOSE-PARKING

Close-parking is a time-honoured winter tradition. It's the sport where Islanders try to park closest to the doorstep of their designated location, so they don't have to walk in the cold. You leave the car running, while popping in for thirty seconds or minutes.

Look, I'm wearing pyjama pants and my brother's peewee hockey jacket from 1983. Does it look like I planned to stay long?

Note: The correct pyjama pants for out-of-the-house activities are the business casual ones, with the pockets.

Serious competitors challenge themselves to complete an Alpine run. That involves slaloming around downtown blocks countless times, looking for a spot next to the liquor store, which is recognized as the most challenging close-parking zone in the province. If you can pick up a six-pack of Alpine beer without being outside for more than thirty seconds total, you're awarded serious respect from all.

Imagine the rich harvest of fenderbergs you'll build up circling those poorly plowed blocks.

Understanding Island Weather

Prince Edward Islanders experience the weather emotionally.

When the forecast gives the current temperature, we get the mercury reading, sure. But more importantly, we hear what that degree reading actually "feels like." This measurement is captured by a man named Gary MacEwen who lives in a small weather station in Maple Plains. Gary is asked to go get *The Guardian* newspaper in his ill-fitting bathrobe and then to report his sensations.

Gary doesn't use Environment Canada's clinical weather terms like "isolated showers." He registers the emotional impact of the precipitation and relays back that "It's spitting" or that "We're getting a bit of dirt." Gary invented the contorted face Islanders make when walking directly into a cold drizzle.

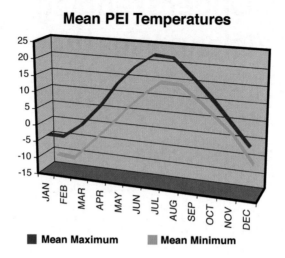

Mean PEI Temperatures

■ Mean Maximum   ■ Mean Minimum

With all these weather fluctuations, it's important to see the broader picture for temperature change across the year. I have graphed the mean temperature changes for PEI, month-over-month. By "mean," I'm saying that the temperatures are mathematically averaged, and also that they are by-and-large unpleasant.

They range from a mean minus eleven degrees in January to a mean minus seven degrees in December, with a blip in the middle that we call "summer," out of force of habit.

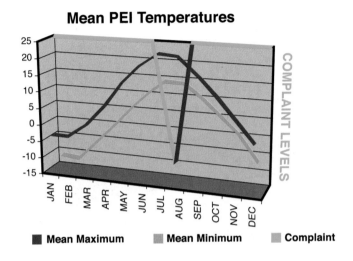

Mean PEI Temperatures

■ **Mean Maximum**   ■ **Mean Minimum**   ■ **Complaint**

What becomes very interesting is cross-indexing levels of Complaint on the Island. Levels of Complaint dance along at nationally high levels for most of the year.

If Islanders lacked the weather as an outlet for this abundant natural resource, social scientists speculate that we might finally turn on each other.

But these levels of Complaint take a nosedive on July 14, a special point that needs analysis. This is Island summer – a bright, fleeting window open for one to two days. In this special time, if one Islander asks another, "How's it going?" the answer will come across as "Can't complain."

Mean PEI Complaint Levels

Can't Complain (1-2 Days)

All conversation will pretty much grind to a halt there. An Islander might attempt to complain, only to have it come out as dry-heaves, as if the saliva itself evaporated under the unfamiliar yellow rays.

Not to worry. For the other 364-ish days of the year, Islanders very much can complain, and will continue to, until you cross the street muttering something about needing to go pick up the kid at daycare.

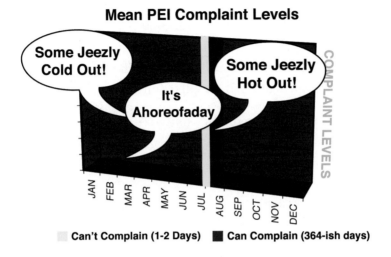

Mean PEI Complaint Levels

The Complaint takes on a few permutations. A short red zone extends from late July to a point halfway through the annual Gold Cup and Saucer parade in mid-August, when the hot times shut down abruptly. In this red zone, an Islander might share the observation that it is "Some jeezly hot out."

This utterance can be accompanied by shirt-flapping but not short-wearing. Adult Islanders don't risk shorts, having had their mammals scared back into the hole too many times by late spring gusts.

In an earlier blue zone of Complaint, the response phrase alters only slightly, into "Some jeezly cold out" or the more personalized "She's some desperate cold out." It's around March that emotions get most strained. We talk about the weather like a bitter former lover, spitting dirty spray over the springtime of our affections.

You might even hear "It's ahoreofaday" muttered under the breath, to no one in particular.

Storm Cancellations

Here are this morning's storm announcements.

- The City of Charlottetown has closed all non-essential services, until 1:00 PM. "Non-essential" covers just about everything, except police, fire, Tim Horton's, and parking tickets to your snow-encased vehicles.

- Despite suboptimal conditions, Shoppers Drug Mart is still open. Do you collect sub-Optimal points? Here are 10,000 for you, for risking deadly roads to buy skin cream 'n' chips.

- Maritime Electric is working to restore electricity to 6,000 customers. Workers are shimmying up icy poles in ninety-kilometre-per-hour gusts. So those of you facing a full hour without power, don't worry. You'll soon be able to recharge Facebook services and resume complaining about the weather.

- Island Hypnosis still closed today. I've been asked to snap my fingers, to release those barking like dogs since Monday afternoon.

- RCMP is urging Island motorists to stay off the roads, because ... Permission to speak freely? You're not good drivers under the best conditions.

- O'Leary is simply closed. Oh really? Yes, O'Leary, really.

- This just in. All provincial civil services closed for the day, including liquor stores. You heard correctly. Be prepared for a good forty-eight-hour look at your family, unfogged by that Bailey's coffee of yours.

- Walk-in clinics closed for the evening. So, this time, the reason you're outside a closed door for four hours with a feverish baby is that there's not really a clinic.

- Atlantic Veterinary College Outpatients is operating on a two-hour delay. So Piddles the Shih Tzu is going to have to deal with human-style wait times, for once. Next time I need a clinic in this province, I'm pinning on a fake tail, saying woof, and heading for the vet.

- Government services at Access PEI are inaccessible today. If you're scheduled for a driver's exam this morning, you will be automatically awarded your license if you can get to Access PEI. Leave a Post-It note as proof. Congrats.

- Waste Watch collections not happening. Those blue bags you carefully sorted and hauled through drifts? Being separated by crows and scattered across your community by the merciless winds.

- Island Storm basketball games cancelled by Island Storm weather, in a polar vortex of self-reference. The Confederation Bridge is closed to high-sided vehicles, and the players are too tall.

- All PEI schools closed. Again. Just closed. For good. There will be a further announcement at 10:30, speculating on the future direction of surplus buildings and students.

- And at this point in an endless winter, I am officially on a system-wide shutdown. I will make a further announcement at 11:00 AM, to my wife and baby.

RIVER RHINO TOUR OF CHARLOTTETOWN

Hello, ladies and gentlemen. Welcome aboard the River Rhino, the only vehicle as ungainly on land as it is on the water.

After a recent performance review, today is my last day working as a tour guide aboard the River Rhino. So I'm going to treat you to an extra-truthy sightseeing tour of my hometown, Charlottetown.

We're coming up on Province House, which is where the Fathers of Confederation first met in 1864, which is why PEI is called the Birthplace of Canada.

Actually, nothing got signed here. They agreed to meet again. I'll allow a moment for your mind to be blown. So it's more the Birthplace of Committee Work. Which, for a country like Canada, is still very significant.

Sorry to disappoint our American visitors. This place is not where Canada defeated the Queen in battle. Canadian history is not that revolutionary. A Canadian license plate would never declare, "Live free or die," like New Hampshire's. Maybe something like "Leave well enough alone."

Let's inch away from the British, across a century or more, and see if they even notice we're gone.

How do I know so much about Confederation? Well, I was a teenage Father of Confederation for a summer, dressed in nineteenth-century costume, though I was barely nineteen myself. Let me tell you, when you wear wool during August, you smell historically accurate.

Oh, the historic sights I did see, strolling about Ye Olde Charlottetown. The merchants of lower Queen Street, whose dry goods trade hasn't changed for decades.

Here's the legendary Beaton's Wholesale, featuring the PEI Mussel Shirt, which has hung in that exact same window for three decades. Wouldn't you love to see that shirt wrapped around the muscles of a PEI man?

PEI men are a lot like PEI mussels. We're cheap, available, and you'll get used to the look of us.

+ If wearing any type of spongy, flexible shoes (i.e.: flip flops or Crocs) please take the stairs or elevator.

Speaking of time standing still, don't miss the downtown Shops of Confederation Court Mall. It's your chance to ride the Island's only escalator. Naturally, you're hesitant to climb aboard such cutting-edge technology.

Don't worry about being run through like a cheese grater. They've posted a helpful set of directions, at both bottom and top, about how to ride an escalator. No lie.

Most important of all, rule number two: Don't get on wearing your Crocs.

If you're still wearing Crocs out in public to shop, I hope the escalator sucks them off your feet for you. They look like salad spinners, and no one has the heart to tell you.

Now we turn the tour north into the hardscrabble heart of Charlottetown. The boulevard of broken dreams, University Avenue.

University Avenue accepts the contradictions of modern life. The collisions that happen when you take your hands off the urban planning wheel, and let the chip trucks fall where they may.

Look at this yin-yang combo under one roof. Karate. Yoga. You'd want to make sure that you were going to class on the right day. "I salute the light within … Sweet chakras, what's with the chop to the head?"

"Damn, it's Wednesday. Namaste, and my mistake. Please stop kicking so I have a moment to roll up my little mat."

While we're on the subject of chops, stop in next door to the Queen Street Meat Market, located right on University Avenue, as one would expect. Where else would it be? You'll be put nose to the grindstone with the finest in local delicacies, as advertised in the classifieds. Lots of eels, large quantity of cod cheeks, back off chicken thighs, or let the kiddos choose something from the big salty aquarium of corned beef.

This is great food. Go on a Queen Street diet for a couple of weeks and wait for the compliments to roll in. "Look at you, packed into those slacks, like a couple cod cheeks and an eel."

Now it's time to get off the Rhino and go walk the streets of Charlottetown on your own. Anybody gives you trouble, just say "Back off, chicken thighs" and try to act local.

The Past Positioning System

Heck, yes, I can point you to a grocery store. You should check out the Big New Sobeys, right by the Little Old Superstore.

But sorry, put away your cellphone with that Global Positioning System. I can only give you directions using the Past Positioning System. Those are directions based on landmarks that aren't here anymore. That's the only way we know how to give directions in Charlottetown.

So you're starting out near the Big New Superstore, what people still call the Kmart parking lot, which hasn't been the case for twenty years.

Head up University Avenue until you see the Towers Mall with no Towers store in it. Zellers came in, then Target, and both are now gone.

The Towers Mall is right across from the Shoppers Drug Mart where the Pizza Hut used to be.

Right after that, you go through the Peter Pan intersection, that doesn't connect with the Peter Pan drive-in anymore, because that refused to grow up and closed. And then you'll see the Big New Sobeys, right across the road from Slick's Place.

Construction continues on the buildings across from Slicks and down from the cinemas.

Construction continues on the buildings across from Slicks and down from the cinemas.

Major retail project on schedule

You don't know who Slick is? He's only the best-known bootlegger within range of the Avenue. Yes, I said best-known bootlegger. Everyone knows that.

When announcing the construction of the Big New Sobeys, the *Guardian* newspaper's business section still had to inform people that the building site was "across from Slick's," so they'd know where it actually was.

Department of Highways put in a new four-way stop light, with a turn lane, in case Slick ever wanted to open a drive-thru. Now that's forward thinking.

New grocery stores and bootlegging, discussed cheek-by-jowl in our business section. You think that's a contradiction?

Welcome to Charlottetown, the Birthplace of Contradiction. You've truly arrived.

If PEI Ruled the World: Whazzisface-book

PEI is where privacy comes to retire.

The Island only has a part-time privacy commissioner, because there is so little of the stuff to look after. She needs to supplement her income by legislating other semi-existent areas like unicorn farming and leprechaun housing.

Facebook is the last place to find out anything private about an Islander. Long before that, it's out through the traditional grapevine, hanging like underwear in the breeze. Let it flap. Everybody already knows the colour.

If PEI ruled the world, Facebook would be used how Islanders use it: as a flashcard game for matching up faces and names. We look up the faces of people we already know everything else about, except their names. The network will be called Whazzisface-book. As in, "Is that old Whazzisface out with Whodya-callit there, getting up to godknowswhat?"

Whazzisface-book would help answer questions like that.

"Is that Whazzisface who gave me locker-room wedgies, now opening his own fitness place?" Yup, one and the same. Twenty-five years later, I won't be joining his health program. Easy enough. Whazzisface-book will be a continually updated junior high yearbook – very helpful in a province where you have to continuously exist next to people from junior high.

Another aspect of Whazzisface-book that would change is how things get liked. In usual Facebook, you can only like things or *not* like them. That system is too simple for the rich stew of emotions an Islander feels when receiving someone else's good news.

One of the problems of social networking is that it allows other people to stuff their self-congratulatory bouquets in our faces.

In a small place like PEI, every flower that sticks its stem higher is sucking up the rain meant to fall on the rest of us. Over decades, the Island has developed a set of verbal gardening tools for plucking back the petals of taller flowers. They're more nuanced than like-me or like-me-not, offering a full spectrum of emotions from the passive through to the aggressive.

Whazzisface-book would incorporate these interface controls.

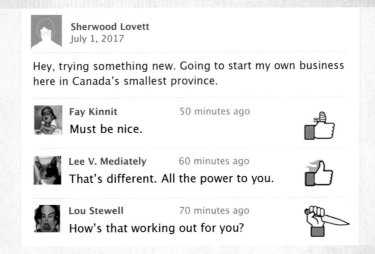

Sherwood Lovett
July 1, 2017

Hey, trying something new. Going to start my own business here in Canada's smallest province.

Fay Kinnit	50 minutes ago	
Must be nice.		

Lee V. Mediately	60 minutes ago	
That's different. All the power to you.		

Lou Stewell	70 minutes ago	
How's that working out for you?		

The more passive commenter might greet good news with "Must be nice." That's an expression directed mainly at oneself, tamping down self-hurt, naming the exact emotion one is not managing to display.

The aggression can be torqued up with a "That's different" or a power-sucking "All the power to you." Both imply that the receiver of the comment is pursuing an off-the-grid path, different from what any right-thinking individual might choose to do.

The knives come out with "How's that working out for you?" The question both suspects and expects an answer.

Because if you want to cut someone down to size, is there any more precise way than just handing over the knife and asking someone to prune where they're already withering?

FAMILY IS A
SENTENCE

The Debate: Is It Important to Know Our Ancestry and Family Trees?

My answer: No, not necessary knowledge, beyond a certain point.

When I was eight years old, I went to a wake, because that's what you do as a family during Island winters. As I passed through the lineup, an older nun looked me in the eye and asked, "Now, who was your mother before she married and had you?"

It took me a full minute to figure out the question. "Before she married and had me, she wasn't my mother. I wasn't even zero yet and didn't know the lady."

In Island conversations, I get asked genealogical details as an opening question more often than humane greetings, like "What's your name?"

In urban areas, when someone says, "Who's your daddy?" you're about to get pinned down, for wrestling or heaven knows what. Around the Island, when someone asks, "Who's your father?" they're also trying to pin you down. It makes me feel I'm not even a person. No, I'm just a chromosomal link in a genetic jigsaw puzzle, standing here while this genius snaps it together.

I'm not embarrassed by my family ties. I just don't want to be lashed down by them.

My approach to ancestry is what I call the Luke Skywalker principle. You should not be exposed to so much family history that you live in fear of becoming your father. On the other hand, you should not given so little family history that you risk marrying your sister.

That's the practical reason to know your family tree. So it doesn't grow in a wreath-like direction. Find a dateable person on eHarmony. com, do a quick cross-index on Genealogy.ca, and you're good to go.

In real life, genealogy is a hobby pursued by those who have already bored away immediate family members.

Every summer on PEI, my parents got a knock on the door from some long-lost cousin, ready for one-sided conversation and to eat their own weight in Nanaimo bars. "I'm your third cousin twice-removed, from Virginia." I have 300 cousins on the Island already, and due to the current volume of cousins, we're not accepting any new applications. Time for a third removal, from the living room.

Besides, ancestry flattens the truth, because we want to flatter ourselves.

People are always busy tracing themselves back to William the Conqueror. You never hear anyone bragging that their ancestry goes back to Eric the Goat-Tickler. Or Tim the Stainer of Pants, who sharted his tunic at the first sight of the enemy cresting the hill at the Battle of Hastings.

Funny, before Tim stained his pants and fled in shame, the military records state that he led well. Ledwell. Oh sweet crap.

Family reunions are hot-air balloons borne aloft with half-truths, starting with the words "family" and "union." Just a bunch of strangers slinging around phrases like, "You have your grandfather's eyes, and your great-aunt's nose." Pleasant message for an eight-year-old. Your face is a mutant organ farm, growing replacement parts for your decrepit relatives.

In coats of arms, the animals are all mutants, combining the worst parts of otherwise fine animals. An eagle's head with lion's claws, stuck on the body of a dolphin.

That's what you'll find if you look too closely at your family tree: peckerheads clawing at each other, spouting air out their blowholes, all the way down.

When it comes to ancestry, my response is DNA. "Do Not Ask."

The Ancient Arms of

LEDWELL

Good Old-Fashioned Food

In my house growing up, food came served with a set of traditional sayings. My parents gleaned these sayings from upbringings in rural Island villages and used them unsparingly at the table. Didn't like something that was served? "All the more for the rest of us." Some food fell on the floor? "Jump on him when he's down."

I'm not kidding. When food went airborne, we kids would parrot back this last gem, learned from my mother. Not a sentiment you should say out loud, in this century, in civilized company. We didn't think about it.

The sayings conveyed a clear message. Food is scarce, and there's no room for fussy pants. Eat what's put in front of you. Otherwise, it will be gobbled up by a scabbier mongrel in this pack of carrion-feeders.

It's not that we lacked for food. But for my parents, food had been so long stewed in Depression-era values, they could never regain the innocence that boiled away. As kids, we didn't really get it, coming from a carpeted living room with an Atari, VCR, and hot-air popcorn poppers.

For my father, the turnip possessed a moral value. "When I was growing up, we thought turnip tasted like ice cream," he would say, solemnly, while serving steaming yellow lumps with an ice-cream scoop. We were not fooled. We just heard that as, "I never tasted ice cream growing up." We didn't lack for empathy, but the generation gap was too big to bridge.

Years later, an Austrian friend and chef said of the turnip, "In Vienna, we call those rutabagas and feed them to the pigs." Just like I'd always suspected.

I would hate to hear what my Austrian friend would say about what we called Vienna sausages. They also held gourmet status for my father, who liked them slathered in yellow mustard. They are truncated hot dogs, canned in their own cold dead jelly. Probably made from the snouts of turnip-fed Viennese pigs.

Taste was governed by tradition. When Saturday night came, it was time for baked beans. The homemade variety, not the canned sort that came with the one fatty piece of legally sufficient pork.

Everything happened in perfect order. As a parent, why wouldn't you pack six children full to the brim with beans at 7:00 PM on a Saturday night? Then fourteen hours later, trundle them into a sport van, drive to a Catholic church, and seat them together smackdab up front?

Sometime around the second reading, the words "church pew" took on a distinct second meaning for us.

All of these food delicacies were available for purchase at our local grocery store, the Co-op (pronounced *kw-op*). And if the Co-op didn't have them, we didn't need them. The Co-op didn't upsell on the leading national, or the tasty, brand of anything. Instead, there were big practical tubs of foodstuffs, which went a long way because they weren't delicious enough to provoke unrequired eating.

I'm still convinced that Co-op margarine and Co-op ice cream were the same damn thing. They were both oily vats. The only difference was that one got kept in the freezer, shot through with a vein of cocoa tar that Co-op passed off as "ripple."

My father reserved the job of picking ice cream for himself and bought whatever ice cream was on sale. He was poorly qualified for the job of selecting a good one. He thought the stuff tasted like turnip.

He often chose grapenut, which interlarded the ice cream with some sort of semi-edible wood pellet. I still don't know what a grapenut is. I once looked under a grape, and they don't have any.

If dessert was this conflicted, you can only suppose how morally charged breakfast could get. In winter, we waited for the school bus in the howling rural winds.

So each cold morning, my father ensured we were properly sandbagged down with something called Red River Cereal. Before boiling, the grist looked like what you'd put under tires, to get a school bus off an icy patch. My father said the hot cereal would stick to our ribs. I was an adult before it fully exited my system.

When spring returned, our bowls would shift to our other breakfast ration, Co-op wheat puffs. This cereal had all the flavour and moisture of styrofoam pellets and must have served a practical purpose as the packing materials for the decent-tasting cereals.

Given that the wheat puffs were so unpalatable, it was fortunate that they were only sold in a Red Cross airlift–sized bag. The bag was taller than our middle siblings. It immediately crushed our hopes of eating through it any time before winter came again.

Mom would heave the new wheat puff bag across the yard, struggling to angle it properly through the door. I can remember thinking, "What misfortune has visited my family to deserve this allotment? Did a helicopter drop it for us?"

The only motivation to keep eating through the wheat puffs was the long-promised prize at the bottom of the bag. One plastic soldier. Sergeant Wheat Puff, his resolute face the same green colour as his uniform and weapons. You had to be inspired by the way Sarge held his courage together, stranded and buried in his wheatdust outpost.

We're coming to save you, Sergeant. If everyone on this sibling brigade keeps up their cereal-eating pace, without hope or fear, we should reach you in six months. No one gets left behind.

At our eating rate through wheat puff bags, I had it figured that I would be fifty-six years old before I had a decent platoon of those soldiers.

I think my parents secretly admired how we worked together. For them, food was permanently seasoned with the taste of pulling through adversity, and it was clear that the lessons were starting to stick.

The Christmas Wish Book

In 1981, when I was eight years old, the arrival of the Sears Wish Book heralded the official start of the Christmas season. It arrived right on time, the second day of school in sunny September. Sitting in the mailbox as thick and inevitable as biblical prophecy.

After its arrival, my parents tried their best to delay the release of Christmas wishes. We weren't allowed to crack the plastic vac-seal until the day after Halloween.

The Sears Wish Book was the map that unlocked Christmasland. I would squirrel away early mornings with the Wish Book, pen and scissors poised, and concoct a Christmas master plan, complete with first choices and if-then contingencies.

Good thing I had contingency plans. Mom was busy with the other four siblings at the time and must have been slow relaying my 1981 wish list. By the time my list arrived, the standing reserve of Star Wars figures was depleted. That Christmas morning, I didn't get R2-D2 but a lesser, plain-featured cousin called Power Droid, who appeared in the movie for seven seconds, off to the side, and looked like a propane barbecue. You know how Chewbacca gets without his grilled meats at staff events.

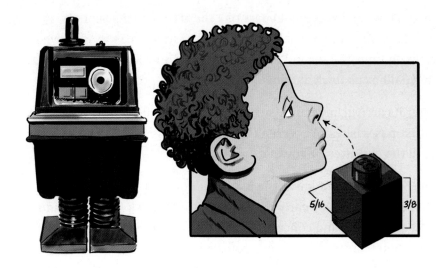

I did get the Lego I'd asked for. Safety standards were different in 1981 and Lego was still shipping the infamous one-pegger piece. The one that's the exact diameter of a younger brother's nostril, as if engineered to go in there. Once slicked, good luck getting that to leggo.

As an eight-year-old, I didn't browse the Wish Book just to receive. It was also a place where I could flip forward to grown-up chapters, picking perfect gifts for Mom and Dad.

I wanted to get my mom the fanciest earrings available. I chose earrings in the same way a brook trout chooses what fishing lures to bite. "If they're plenty shiny, and unnaturally long, I'll be snapping that bling up."

From browsing the Sears Wish Book, I learned that I had much to look forward to when I became an adult man.

Soft, warm TERRY Velour
In a thick, thirsty cotton blend

I could anticipate leisurely weekends with my handsome man friends, standing as a group in our brand-spanking new bathrobes. When I read the words "Terry Velour," I thought they referred to the name of the main guy in the picture.

Nigel, Theodore, Cecil – the whole gang would stay over. We'd laugh together at something just outside the frame, probably a heap of our discarded bathrobes. "Can you believe we sported those frayed, pilly embarrassments so long, waiting for this plush Christmas morning?"

Eventually, I'd meet an attractive woman, through one of our bimonthly co-ed bathwear mixers. I'd know it was her right away, on account of the exact matching bathrobe. And then I'd finally discover what was lies underneath that thick, thirsty cotton blend.

Snuggle up in a snug sack
28⁰⁰

A wallpaper-print challis nightie. The kind of nightie that walls off any suggestive drifts with six inches of cotton batting and declares bed, bath, and nothing beyond.

And then I in my terry velour and my Wish Book partner in her snug sack would settle ourselves in for a long winter's nap.

PEI by the Numbers

A6 The Guardian
Tuesday, April 15, 2008

The Island way not always the best way

I grew up believing that Prince Edward Island is the best place in the world. I may not have experienced a representative sample of enough other places to make such a statement beyond a doubt. But in my heart of hearts, I believed the Island to be the best, and I left concerns about scientific sampling right there.

So it always causes me great shock when I'm greeted on the doorstep with bad news about the Island. Sometimes, this bad news is writ large in our own newspaper of record, *The Guardian*. I'll never forget this heavy-set headline from 2008. The assertion shook me to my core.

How are we supposed to conduct our lives if the Island way is not always the best way? If I want action, I suppose I'll just call 1-800 numbers for government help like everyone else. I used to think the best way was to call my elected member at home, right at dinnertime, and ask when the plow would be around. That's not the best way, any-more, apparently.

I might as well start acting like someone born in Barrie, Ontario.

77 OTHER AREAS

Yard Sale
Mother is in home, Kids in Alberta, stuff must go. Crystal, china , furniture, curtains, something for everyone. ▪▪▪ ▪▪▪▪▪ ▪▪▪ ▪▪▪, Canoe Cove. Follow Rte 19A. Look for signs.

Like it or not, it is unquestionable that the Island way is currently taking its lumps. When I really want to take the pulse of the province, I read the newspaper from back to front. Because it is in the fine print, the true classifieds, where one can read the current shape of people's lives. How are Island lives getting matched and dispatched, in as few paid words as possible?

This classified, for example, is not tip-toeing around the issues. Ma is humming in a corner suite, leaving behind an army of Royal Doulton figurines no one wants to adopt. The next generation has lit out for Alberta, abandoning their milkcrates full of student-loan-bought books. Now, this family archive is getting pitched into the front yard, slapped with masking-tape prices.

The ad clearly says: Take this landfill from my sight before the drizzle gets it. Don't any waste time feeling bad. My thankless Calgary children certainly didn't.

> In comparison, P.E.I. has lower partici-
> pation scores in activities such as going
> to zoos, aquariums, botanical gardens,
> art galleries and museums with an aver-
> age about 12 per cent lower than the rest
> of the country.
>
> The main reason these scores are low
> might be because these things aren't
> readily available to Islanders, which is
> something some people are striving for.

The truth of our struggle is there in the numbers, as much as it comes written in the words. Quite regularly, Prince Edward Island ranks near the bottom of province-by-province rankings. Arriving unvarnished in the newspaper, these discouraging statistics broadside us in black and white.

We need to take a good, hard look and ask ourselves, "Why do we have lower participation scores in activities such as going to zoos, aquariums, and botanical gardens?" Is it related to the fact that these facilities aren't available to Islanders? You can spend an awful long drive with the family, casting about for a PEI zoo. I thought I found a zoo once, but it was just a hobby farm with a really ugly horse.

We try our best. In Grade Four PEI French, some of the first words I learned were the names of zoo animals. *La giraffe, l'éléphant, l'hippopotame.* But on the Island, I did not get equal opportunity to use this vocabulary regularly, as we lack the zoo. I could use the negative tense, which we only learned later. "*Il n'y a pas de giraffe ni de hippopotame. Zut alors. Ce n'est pas formidable.*"

Keep long-form survey,
P.E.I. municipalities urge

Census Canada 2011

Short Form Census Version

1. Name: ▶

2. **Are you dead yet?** ☐ Yes ☐ No
(Please check all that apply)

To build our Island society and face our shared challenges, we need good numbers. We need the long-form Canadian census, which provided an accurate snapshot of how many people are in our Island municipalities. Recent censuses have stopped looking into communities of 25,000 people or less, which – let's be honest – rides the cut-offs too high for places like Prince Edward Island.

The most recent 2011 short-form census, pictured above in its entirety, was not adequate. It was very efficient to complete, I'll give it that. If it's not returned with a checkmark, that person must be deceased. But that is not enough information about Prince Edward Islanders to know and to grow our society. Some Islanders are just sound sleepers, and a poke in the census would let us know more about them.

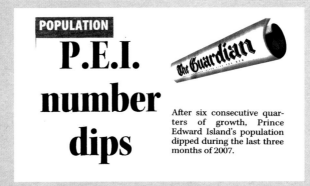

POPULATION

P.E.I. number dips

The Guardian

After six consecutive quarters of growth, Prince Edward Island's population dipped during the last three months of 2007.

Professionals from Statistics Canada can – and indeed should – continue to examine our province every quarter of the year. Because across the span of three mere months, the PEI population can undergo sudden and seismic shifts. Our Island population is that strangely sensitive.

Consider for example the last quarter of 2007, a remarkable historical time now referred to as "The Dip." After dancing along with six consecutive quarters of growth, the Island experienced a sudden and unexplained population crash, as registered by the hair-trigger demographic devices at Statistics Canada.

> In a report released last week, Statistics Canada said P.E.I.'s population now stands at 139,089, a drop of 0.01 per cent.
> In October, the Island's population stood at 139,103.

At the start of that quarter, the Island was bustling along with 139,103 people. Then, our population figures mysteriously entered into a 0.01 per cent barrel roll, free-falling and finally bottoming out at 139,089 people. Out of nowhere, the Island was missing fourteen people.

Statistics Canada admits that there is a margin for error. At least two of those people might have been in the bathroom at time of count. Still, it's daunting to consider that the Island can suddenly just disappear a baker's dozen worth of people, give or take. These kinds of population challenges must be met square on.

It's not an insurmountable gap, Islanders. We all know a relative, friend, or spouse who has moved off-Island in recent years. Let's work together to bring at least fourteen of them back, to return our population to full health.

Here's what I've been doing. I cut good news out of our local newspaper and then mail copies to my dear departed loved ones. Once they see the good things happening on the Island, in real actual newsprint, no doubt that I'll lure at least one or two back. We all need to do our part to help replace the fourteen that can go missing, from time to time.

For today, I'll demonstrate this good news strategy with real estate. I always start with real estate. These actual clippings speak volumes. I have countless friends and siblings, in Toronto and Calgary, whose backs are bent under the weight of six-figure house prices. What a relief to know that they can retreat back to PEI and live in a castle for a fraction of those hefty sums.

JUST LISTED

North River Road one word
ELIGENT. Phone

Look at this majestic home, pulled right from the real estate listings. Only one word describes this palace. "Eligent." It escapes description in existing words. It's one part eligible, and one part intelligent. That is a hard blend of qualities to find in a datable man in Charlottetown. You might as well look for an eligent house on your own, and start building your new life from there.

Not everyone wants to live in a big city like Charlottetown. I love living in rural PEI, where the curious breezes sport new smells every day. When considering rural life, I'd recommend looking at the lot moreso than the current house on it. Maybe the house is a fixer-upper, maybe it's a tumbler-downer. Concentrate on the lot.

In this tempting ad, the house is on a "small pie shaped lot." When purchasing a small pie-shaped lot, take my insider's advice. Buy one of the pie-shaped lots where the crust side is facing the road.

Then, everyone driving along will get the impression that you have a huge spread. It's only the closer acquaintances whom you invite around back for a deck barbecue who will realize that your backyard is pointy.

By then, they know you well, and what's the sense of continuing to try to impress?

Former Store With Owners
Suite & Rental Apt. Could Be
Easily Converted Back To Store.
Call _____ #561

When I try to lure friends and relatives back to the Island, some chime back with objections. I'm sure you'll hear some of the same ones. "If I came back to the Island, what would I do for work?" Start a business, I suggest, if you can't find something in your field. "That's a ton of investment, hours, and risk," they reply.

So buy a former store with owners, for crying out sake. You just purchase the whole shooting match. Betty and Irv, they've been working there and living in back for the last thirty-eight years. The last thing they want to do is move. You just sit in your separate living quarters, watching the hockey game on Saturday night, while seventy-year-old Betty and Irv are out front slinging the cola and Cheetos to the neighbours. That's an ideal package.

Downtown Ch'town
Newly renovated 2 Bdrm
duplex. F/S, Dishwasher,
Microwave fireplace,
jacuzzi
$800/mth unheated.

Rather than buying a new place outright, many returning to the Island prefer to rent at first. In that case, you will find yourself dancing squarely in the lap of luxury, surrounded by the most modern of amenities. Apartments in Charlottetown are not the humble garrets of yesteryear, when "heritage" was another way of saying the wiring's not up to code. Consider this apartment as a typical contestant for your attentions. It's got a "microwave fireplace." With one of those units, you can have a full evening by the fire in less than three minutes. Word of caution: Don't wear your yoga pants while sitting close to your microwave fireplace. It'll melt the lulu right onto your lemons. I speak from experience.

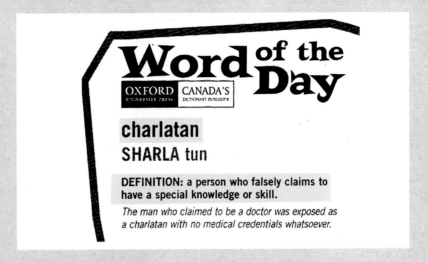

Word of the Day

OXFORD UNIVERSITY PRESS | CANADA'S DICTIONARY PUBLISHER

charlatan
SHARLA tun

DEFINITION: a person who falsely claims to have a special knowledge or skill.

The man who claimed to be a doctor was exposed as a charlatan with no medical credentials whatsoever.

There is usually lots to do in Prince Edward Island, but it does slow down in the winter. During the winter, one of the things I like to do is commit myself to learning the Word of the Day, which arrives in the newspaper.Here's the wonderful word "charlatan." What's wonderful about the word is that I do not much need it at all in Charlottetown (which is also pronounced *char-la-tan*). If you are a person who "falsely claims to have a special knowledge or skill," you may fool a couple of people. But then word about your amateur roofing services travels around town really fast. Islanders pass around negatives as efficiently as the back-end of a battery.

It's a charlatan-proofing quality, which our small community possesses in abundance.

Unlocked cars prime targets for thieves at Christmas

City Police conducting random vehicle checks

Another main reason our community is so safe for people coming back is the efforts of the Charlatan police. They are always engaging in new forms of community policing to thwart the ne'er-do-wells.

Pictured here is a representative headline from the paper, describing a forward-thinking police initiative to stand on guard at Christmas. Unfortunately, in our trusting community, Islanders leave cars unlocked and become targets for Grinches looking to pick Whoville clean of presents.

Picture yourself ditty-bopping through the mall, oblivious with Christmas cheer. Meanwhile, the City Police are busy as elves in the parking lot, doing secret good deeds. They're checking random car doors to see if they're locked. That's a condition that someone should seize upon, and quickly.

"If we find your vehicle unlocked and there are Christmas presents or other valuables inside we leave a ticket on your vehicle,"

Here's how the program works. If your car doors aren't locked, the officer leaves a non-fine ticket on the windshield, as a visible reminder to all that the doors of this vehicle are open.

That way, the charlatans don't have to waste all the livelong day jim-jammering every car door in the mall parking lot. It saves the occasional broken window, because who the dickens would go to all that effort, with these well-labelled presents to choose from.

They can just look for the tickets. "Hey, ticket there, ticket here, ticket on that Toyota Tercel two across."

At this point, I believe we've made a compelling case through the clippings, in smudge-resistant black and white, that Prince Edward Island is a safe and trusting place to make your life. Homes are handsome, affordable, and always being looked into by your neighbours.

I suspect that if we all committed to send off these good news stories to loved ones, we'd be back up the missing people within the next four to six months.

Governments give Island businesses boost to succeed

"We are 140,000-odd people. That market is not big enough for our products. We need to go outside.

We need to have our elevator pitch ready when we come across someone in a Toronto elevator who might be swayed to move to PEI. They have tall buildings in Toronto, and the elevator ride is long enough to leave an impression.

Our provincial government is already on the job. When they send emissaries outside the province, they have their recruitment message prepared. "We are 140,000 odd people." And if you're an odd person, there's no better place in the world for you than Prince Edward Island.

We're currently short about fourteen people. You have ten more floors down to think about it. Will you join us?

PEI PROS AND CONS: CONCLUSION

PEI Pros and Cons: Conclusion

Some Islanders say the glass is half full. Some Islanders say the glass is half empty. Other Islanders say, "Look at you. Needing a glass."

"Why not drink from the glass it came in? It's called a bottle, with a special little tunnel that leads to your face. I'm not turning on the dishwasher for the likes of you."

The Island's a funny place.

PEI Pros

You know people from way back in high school.

Everytime I shop at the Co-op, I'm always in the top 5 sexiest people there.

Fiddlers keep everything together with a wink and a nod and nothing ever written down.

PEI Cons

If I want to buy a car, and not deal with salesmen who bullied me in high school, I have to go to Moncton.

We have a rapidly aging population.

Government is run like fiddling. Wink, nod, nothing ever written down.

PEI Pros

If you don't like it here, you know where the bridge is, son of a biscuit eater.

Islanders will never leave you all alone.

I'm so close to my family here.

I feel wrapped by a huge quilt.

PEI Cons

Islanders are too sensitive to criticism.

Islanders will *never* leave you alone.

Oh God, I'm too close to my family here.

I feel trapped by a huge quilt.

Being an Islander is getting handed down a woollen sweater with sentimental meaning. It's tight and knit and just a quarter-inch away from unwearable. But just you try and give it away.

And so you stand there and hold the smile for the picture. Belonging, surrounded, and itchy, wondering just how much longer you can keep it on.

Acknowledgments

Thanks to my editor and agent David Malahoff. For the last nine years and continuing, David has been my sounding board when I want to know what's working. Thanks for opening the attachments.

Thanks to my sister Jane for her sharp edits to the manuscript. She's a copy editor with whom you don't want to mess.

Thanks to Terrilee Bulger of Acorn Press, for her support on the manuscript. Life was full the last couple years, and she understood (or at least accepted) when timelines got pushed.

Thanks to my Ledwell and Costello families, who are appreciative and loving supporters of my odd enterprises.

Thanks to Mark Haines, who has been an inspiring collaborator through several summers of the show *The Island Summer Review*. It's motivating to perform with someone who, after four decades, brings such joy and invention to each performance.

Thanks to Melanie and Kris Taylor, who built and created Harmony House Theatre, where I've been fortunate to develop shows. Partnership with Harmony House has helped sustain me, in several ways, during the writing of the book. I appreciate the audiences and alchemy of the place.

Thanks to the talented artist Jeff Alward for the uncanny cover design of the book and a couple of creative illustrations inside. Your cover was excellent motivation to finish the book before my son Nate changed his looks.

Thanks to Richard Side, Anna Bonokoski, and Steve Patterson at CBC Radio's *The Debaters*. I know there are plenty of talented people you could call without the extra flight arrangements and hotel nights. Thanks for still calling.

Thanks to CBC PEI in Charlottetown, for hosting me as a columnist and for helping spread word about creative projects.

Thanks to *The Guardian* newspaper, for allowing your actual clippings to appear in these pages. Your newsprint captures the workings of the Island mind so perfectly, and the clippings are a channel to – and not the butt of – the joke. I hope reprinting is a sincere form of flattery.

And thanks to you reader, for picking this up. It's a vote to continue.